SILENCING YOUR INNER SABOTEUR

2nd Edition

SILENCING YOUR INNER SABOTEUR

2nd Edition

Sherry Peters

© 2013 Sherry Peters

All rights reserved. No portion of this book may be reproduced by any process or technique, without the express consent of the author, except in the case of brief quotations embodied in critical articles and reviews.

First edition: e-book, July 2011

DwarvenAmazon Press
http://sherrypeters.wordpress.com

Printed in the U.S.A.

Peters, Sherry, 1973 –
Silencing Your Inner Saboteur - 2nd ed.

ISBN: 978-0-9920535-0-5

Author Photo by: Robert J. Sawyer

For
Adria Laycraft

Contents

Acknowledgements 9

Introduction: Second Edition 11

Introduction 15

Chapter 1 19
    What is the Saboteur

Chapter 2 35
    Roots

Chapter 3 49
    The Dominant Voice

Chapter 4 63
    Acknowledge our Fears

Chapter 5 79
    Whispers of Sweet-Nothings

Chapter 6 95
    The Physical Manifestation or The Symptoms

Chapter 7 117
    What's in a Name?

Chapter 8 129
    Challenge Yourself

Chapter 9 145
    Silence the Inner Saboteur

Chapter 10 159
    Keeping the Saboteur Silent

Conclusion 171

Appendices 177
    Prioritization
    Time Management
    Creating a Workable Plan

Resources 203

About the Author 209

Acknowledgements

I want to give special thanks to everyone who helped me Silence my Inner Saboteur, and with this project in particular. Specifically: Anne Harris, Leslie Davis Guccione, Jeanne Cavelos, Susan Sielinski, Barbara Barnett-Stewart, Jeff Lyman, all of my Odyssey 2005 classmates, and all my fellow SHUers past, present, and future.

Lane Robins, I can't thank you enough for setting me on this path of discovery. You have helped me more than you will ever know.

I especially want to thank Adria Laycraft, Bev Geddes, Gerald Brandt, and Robert J. Sawyer; my family Barb, Jake, Darrell, Cheryl, Katarina, Angelica, and Thomas. I am forever indebted to you for your support.

To all of you, I couldn't have written this book without you!

Introduction: Second Edition

I am pleased to bring you the second edition of *Silencing Your Inner Saboteur*. A lot has changed since the first edition was published.

In my practice as a Success Coach, it is my job to help my clients uncover and explore the inevitable objections which arise as they strive toward achieving their goals. As coaches, we call these obstacles "gifts" because when they arise, they provide an opportunity to go deeper with our clients, often resulting in wonderful moments of transformation. Everyone experiences some kind of resistance or blockade halting their progress. Whether that goal be weight-loss, changing a career, or becoming a writer, the resistance we experience comes from the same place—the inner saboteur.

I've written this book with writers as the intended audience, but you may find you recognize the work of the saboteur in other areas of your life as well. I know I have, and readers and participants in the workshops I facilitate on this topic have said the same.

I have incorporated my education and experience as a Success Coach, and more of the material from the workshop to expand the chapters from the first edition. Chapters on the four main fears we face when working on a project, challenging ourselves and appendices with additional tools to silence the saboteur have been added.

We begin by identifying what exactly is an inner saboteur and what it is not. In identifying what the saboteur is, we can then make note of what the saboteur says.

Once we identify what the saboteur is, we move on to discuss where the saboteur comes from and how it uses its birth from negative past experiences and comments against us. We then take some time on the voices the saboteur uses against us, and in particular its dominant voice and why it chooses that voice most often.

Next we will discuss the four main categories of fear our saboteur uses against us while working on a project, how those fears affect us and how we can work around them or eliminate them.

From there we move on to the sweet-nothings the saboteur likes to whisper to us in an effort to lure us away from our writing. It is important to note that what we believe are sweet-nothings may not be. They may be a very real need. We will discuss how to determine if they are sweet-nothings or if they are a real need, and if they are a sweet-nothing, how to make them work to our advantage, not the saboteur's.

Then we'll spend some time discussing the physical symptoms, the physical, external signs and outcomes if we listen to the saboteur; things like writer's block, lack of motivation, and simply not feeling like writing.

By now, we will have a number of tools to recognize and mentally silence the saboteur. The final few chapters will cover more practical and physical ways we can silence the saboteur.

It is important to name the saboteur. Naming the saboteur takes away its power, and the fear of the unknown is no longer valid.

We must also challenge ourselves as writers. Don't be afraid to learn, and to push ourselves. Writing is an on-going learning process. Acknowledging that and developing ourselves as writers gives us power over the saboteur.

The final two chapters will cover other methods and tools we can use to silence the saboteur.

This book is not a guarantee of publication, but if you complete the exercises and learn to silence the inner saboteur, you will get to a place where you are happy with your writing, where you can feel proud of what you have done, that you have done everything you possibly can to make your dream come true.

As a Success Coach, I believe that:
- People make the best choices available to them.
- Everyone is capable of being the best version of themselves.
- People already have all the resources they need within themselves to get whatever they truly want.

These are principles that I apply to my practice as a coach, and to every chapter and exercise in this book. By the end, you too, will see that you have the resources within yourself to silence the saboteur.

Together, we can express ourselves, our creativity, and succeed in writing and silencing the inner saboteur.

Introduction

Welcome to *Silencing Your Inner Saboteur*. This book is designed to help writers of every level to silence their inner saboteur, to identify the voice of their saboteur, recognize the tricks it uses to keep them from achieving their goals, and how to win the battle against it.

Ever since I could hold a pencil, I wanted to write. My loopy scribbles were beautiful cursive writing to me, which I proudly passed to my mom, telling her I'd written her a letter or a story. Whether it was intentional encouragement, or she wanted me to stop interrupting her conversations with family and guests, she'd tell me to write some more. Intentional or not, she did encourage me.

After I'd learned how to read and write—I was probably age 6 or 7—I began to write chapter books. Of course, a chapter was a sentence long, so to fill up the rest of the page, I drew the illustrations. At least I did on some of the pages. I was far more interested in the writing so I am sure the pictures stopped. My mom helped me make covers for these chapter books out of construction paper, stapling the pages together.

It was so much easier to write back then. Nothing stood in my way. I didn't doubt my talent as a writer, I had the books to prove it.

If only the business of writing stayed that easy.

Unfortunately, in our pursuit of publication, of awards, of placing on the bestsellers list, we no longer have the innocence of a child, and the saboteur becomes more vocal, more persuasive, hindering our progress, crushing our hopes and dreams before we being to chase after them.

I wrote for years after high school, but I never felt like I knew enough about the process of writing, or even how to write. I applied to the Odyssey Writing Workshop, seeing it as an amazing six week intensive opportunity to learn a lot of the essentials of writing I'd never had the chance to learn before. I attended Odyssey in the summer of 2005. The workshop, and the director and our instructor, Jeanne Cavelos, gave me the tools and the confidence to know I was going in the right direction with my writing.

In 2007, I began my M.A. in Writing Popular Fiction at Seton Hill University in Greensburg, Pennsylvania, a low-residency program, meaning I was on campus twice a year for one week each time. This was another opportunity to advance my knowledge and skill-set for storytelling, and novel-writing. Seton Hill's Writing Popular Fiction program is an amazing program, with incredible mentors and students, and was a nurturing environment in which we learned from each other. Over the two years I was a student at Seton Hill University, I had plenty of doubt over what I was writing, but there were two incidents which stopped me from writing for long stretches of time. I would force myself to get the pages written each month I needed to turn in for critique, but those pages were less than adequate in content.

Plagued by self-doubt and hatred for what I was writing, contemplating quitting writing all together, I took to my blog and wrote about how my internal critic was being so mean to me. One of the comments I received was from Lane Robins, Class of 1999, of the Odyssey workshop, author of the amazing *Maledecte* and *Kings and Assassins*. What Lane said changed my whole understanding of what was happening, what I was doing to myself. Lane said it didn't sound like it was my inner critic, but a saboteur.

The idea of an inner saboteur has intrigued me ever since that blog post back on August 11, 2008. I have spent a lot of time the last few years paying attention to my thought process as I write. I pay attention to the creative process. When the writing was easier, I asked myself what was going on in my life and what my thought processes were, to make the creativity flow? More important, I began to focus on what my thought processes were when the writing was not flowing, when I didn't want to write, what I was telling myself, what my saboteur was telling me.

As a result, I developed several strategies with which to silence my saboteur, which I will share with you. Along the way, there were a number of books I encountered, which were instrumental in helping me understand the saboteur and how to silence him. I have kept this book and its resources simple and easy to handle, focusing on those I found most helpful.

We will begin by discussing what exactly the saboteur is, then move from identifying the voice of the saboteur, to discussing how the saboteur manifests itself in our lives, and finally on to how to silence it. Everyone's life experience is different. I will be presenting examples and scenarios in each chapter which are intended to start your own thoughts about where you are at. Following each chapter, there is a short exercise to help apply what was discussed.

One of my biggest problems with books on writing is all the exercises they have at the end of each chapter. I always think they take up too much time, time I *should* be spending writing, even if the chapters were useful. All the exercises here are short. Do not spend a lot of time on them. However, they are important to do. I recommend they are best done through journaling, whether that be through your regular journal, pieces of paper stapled together, or if you are brave, a blog, whichever makes you most comfortable. All assignments are of a personal nature and I don't recommend you share them with others unless you feel comfortable doing so. This is about eliminating self-doubt, not creating it.

In acknowledging you have an inner saboteur who needs to be silenced, you have already taken a great leap toward that goal. By the end of this book, you will be well on your way to *Silencing Your Inner Saboteur*.

Without giving your saboteur any more time to meddle with your thoughts, let's begin.

Chapter 1

What is the Saboteur

Chapter 1

What is the Saboteur

Your inner saboteur is the little voice inside your head telling you you can't do something, it's too hard, you are not good enough, nobody wants to read your work, you have nothing valuable to say, you have no ideas, what's the point you messed up today, yesterday, why bother trying, and that you are lazy so obviously you are not a writer, otherwise you'd be writing.

Your inner saboteur is the self-doubt inside you which prevents you from starting a new project, working on a work in progress, or submitting to markets and agents. It is every negative comment you have ever told yourself or thought about yourself. It is every limiting belief. It is the devil on your shoulder and your security blanket. Your inner saboteur criticizes you, berates you, and seduces you.

Some people call this inability to write writer's block. They call the lack of motivation to write procrastination. Writer's block and procrastination are symptoms, not the root of the problem, they are the result of listening to your saboteur.

There are dozens of books with writing exercises and prompts to kick-start you out of your writer's block, to get you writing. There are just as many books on finding time to write, making time to write, and how not to procrastinate. Those books are mere band-aid solutions treating the symptoms of the disease, distracting you from the real problem—your saboteur. They work, but for how long? You can put a band-aid over an open wound, but until you've dealt with the sliver inside, you are not going to heal. You can learn all the time management techniques in the world; you can do all the writing exercises in the world, and they will work for a time, but unless they fit with your writing project, fit into your life, and deal with the underlying issues of what is getting in your way, they are not going to last long-term, ultimately leading to greater frustration with the writing process.

Of course your saboteur is going to promote these temporary solutions, push that it is simply writer's block or procrastination, that you are lazy. Your saboteur doesn't want you looking too close at the real problem because to look closely means you would discover your saboteur, realize that the saboteur is the root of the problem, and would do something about it. That's the last thing he wants. So your saboteur will tell you that if you had one more book on how to write, if you made more time to write, then your problems are solved. And yes, they will be, temporarily. But your saboteur is still there, festering, whispering in your ear.

Don't I mean an internal critic, inner editor, or censor, not a saboteur? To call it a critic, editor, or censor is far too kind for what it is: your inner saboteur. Your inner critic, editor, or censor can be just as harmful as your saboteur, but they can serve to keep you on track if we listen to them at the right time.

Your inner critic is expert at criticizing what you are writing, often demanding perfection. Your critic tends to give you plenty of advice about what is wrong, but is never very helpful. This is particularly harmful when writing early drafts. Jack Heffron, in his book, *The Writer's Idea Book*, calls that voice The Critic. In talking about hearing the voice of The Critic while writing early drafts, he says, "When you hear the voice of The Critic telling you your idea is stupid, your writing dull and pedestrian, tell the voice to wait. He may, indeed, be right. And he will have his turn, you promise, but it's not his turn now." (Heffron, 19). Is there an appropriate time for The Critic to speak? Heffron implies there is. Your critic is allowed to demand perfection during the editing process, not before, and not after. Anything else said which is attributed to The Critic, is really the saboteur.

What about the inner editor? The editor, much like the critic, demands perfection. He is more worried about correcting grammar and typos and formatting rather than letting you move on to the next scene or chapter. Your editor will tell you that a sentence isn't quite right, that maybe you need to insert a comma but then tell you to take it out. He will tell you to take your time, to make sure that each sentence is perfect and exactly what you want to say, and if you can't think of the perfect word for several days, that is just fine. The editor can slow the writing process and can paralyze a writer. Heather Sellers in her book *Chapter after Chapter*, says that the editor has its place in helping you edit. "The Little Editor does mean well. She knows you are terrified of making a fool of yourself, and she's truly trying to help. It's just that the fear she induces is not conducive to writing." (Sellers, 157). Your inner saboteur loves to take advantage of the fear created by the editor, stirring it up, exaggerating it in your mind. When you are editing, that is when you need your editor to help with the grammar, typos, spelling errors, and constructing the perfect sentence, to make your writing the best it can possibly be.

And then there is the other name, the internal censor. My preferred definition of the internal censor is that voice that tells you what to and what not to write, mostly what not to write, telling you to watch what you write, there shouldn't be so many swear words, or explicit sex scenes, or a character with the same color hair as a family member, because your family is reading this and they'll think that character is them. Or that people you know will be reading this and what will they think of you then?

Julia Cameron in *The Artist's Way* spends a fair bit of time discussing the Censor. She describes it as "part of our leftover survival brain. It was the part in charge of deciding whether it was safe for us to leave the forest and go out into the meadow. Our Censor scans our creative meadow for any dangerous beasties. Any original thought can look pretty dangerous to our Censor. . . Who wouldn't be blocked if every time you tiptoed into the open somebody (your Censor) made fun of you?" (Cameron, *Artist's Way*, 13). I agree with Cameron's notion of the censor being afraid of new or creative ideas. It is not the censor who is making fun of you, though. The censor thinks it is only trying to protect you from being laughed at. The censor wants to keep your writing safe and hidden in a drawer, he wants to keep you from writing certain ideas, or from submitting your work because yes, you may receive praise and acceptance, but the risk of potential rejection and mockery is too much for the censor. It is your saboteur who mocks you, who laughs at you because you think you can write and submit and get published. It is your saboteur who laughs at you because he doesn't want you to try. To try means you might succeed and success means your saboteur no longer controls you.

There are times when we need our internal censor. Particularly when we're with other people. But there may be times in our writing as well, when we need to be sensetive to external issues and need to find a way to say things in a more gentle manner than we might otherwise.

The saboteur uses disguises like the editor, critic, and censor; it reminds us of negative experiences we have had, because it wants to keep us where we are. But by keeping us where we are, it is preventing us from growing intellectually and emotionally, and it is preventing us from expressing who we really are.

Your saboteur wants to keep you from following your dreams, achieving your goals, and he—I call the saboteur a he because mine is a he, yours may be a she—will do anything and everything to stop you. Maybe he doesn't want you to be hurt. More likely, he doesn't want you to succeed.

Often the saboteur isn't particularly strong, achieving only a short episode of unhappiness or a few days where you "just don't feel like writing." When we permit those episodes of unhappiness or not writing to linger too long we allow the saboteur to take over, we begin a downward spiral of frustration with ourselves and our situation.

Which leads us to what I like to call:

The Gollum Analogy

I like to compare the inner saboteur to the character Gollum in *The Lord of the Rings* by J.R.R. Tolkien. Gollum is, of course, in the books, but I use the characterization of Gollum in the movies which is a beautiful and vivid interpretation by Peter Jackson.

For those who have not read the books or seen the movies, Sméagol was once a Hobbit who finds the magic ring of the Dark Lord Sauron. This ring is all powerful and Sméagol will do anything to keep it. This ring also provides him with unusually long life. As a result of owning this ring, Sméagol is cast out from his family and his community. He loses all sense of taste and fears the brightness of the sun so he retreats to the darkness of caves, where he forgets who he is. Gollum is the dark part of Sméagol's personality which appears to protect himself and mostly the ring of power. Over the years, Gollum becomes the dominant personality. Like Gollum, the inner saboteur can take over if we give him too much time to play with our confidence.

In *The Two Towers*, the second book and movie in *The Lord of the Rings* trilogy, Sméagol is drawn out from under Gollum's control and the two personalities battle it out, much like we battle our evil inner saboteur.

Tell me if any of the following sounds like something your saboteur has told you:

"You don't have any friends. Nobody likes you. Where would you be without me? I saved us. It was me. We survived because of me."

The above is what Gollum tells Sméagol.

When we hear that voice, when Gollum gets too loud in our heads, telling us "Nobody likes you. You don't have any friends. You survived because of me," that is when the self-doubt sets in, and we start to procrastinate, and our creativity, our writing, is blocked. Gollum is so loud in our heads, we cannot hear our ideas, or the other voice, the one so quiet, saying we can do it, we do have friends, and what we write is worth reading.

Can the Saboteur really be silenced?

The short answer is, "Yes. Absolutely." To do so takes a lot of work and focus.

As you go through this book and as you work on your writing projects, pay attention to your saboteur, and note when it gets loudest. Chances are, it will be loudest when a) you are making great progress; or b) when you are stuck or know something isn't right but can't quite give it a name.

When we are succeeding or on the verge of success, the saboteur will raise objections. An objection is when a part of us (the saboteur) prevents us from doing something, from staying motivated to complete a task, or from experiencing a state that we want. An objection is a negative conclusion that holds a limiting belief in place. It is a "cork in the bottle" that stops the flow of information or a shift into action. Objections are often spoken by parts of us (the saboteur), and spoken in negatives. They become our beliefs and conclusions.

What do I mean by limiting belief? A limiting belief is something negative we believe about others that are unfounded and limits our progress. One example we as writers have: Nobody wants to read what I have to write. How do we know if we haven't tried to submit it anywhere, or even if we write something small and for fun for family and friends? An example we might experience in our day-jobs: There's no way I'm going to get that ergonomic keyboard or some other useful tool for work. These limiting beliefs prevent us from asking for what we want.

Often the saboteur strikes when we emotionally or intellectually know something is wrong. In coaching, we say that everything, every action, when our bodies hurt or our minds or hearts protest, it is because what we are protesting doesn't sit right with us, and that something is important and needs to be looked after. Just as our bodies hurt when something is physically wrong with us, so our creativity protests when something isn't right with what we are writing. Either we have tied things up too neatly to go on; we aren't as in love with the story as we should be; or you have an uneasy feeling about the agent you've queried.

There are other objections as well, the external objections such as: "I really don't know enough about writing," "This isn't commercial enough," "Nobody wants to read this." These objections are often directed at our frustration with the business side of writing and because of that frustration, enforce our negative beliefs about ourselves and our writing.

To silence the saboteur, it is important that we find out what it is objecting to. When we figure out the objections, what the problem is, and what is important to us about that particular objection, we can deal with it. To do so, we need to open up a controlled dialogue with the saboteur.

The saboteur will do anything and everything to stop us from achieving our goals. Why is that? Ask your saboteur. More than likely, it is out of a need to protect us from getting hurt should we be rejected or never make it to the level we would think of as success. That's very noble and indeed well intentioned. Ask yourself: What would hurt more, quitting now and giving up on my dreams, or pushing through the years of rejection and waiting, never getting published, but knowing I tried everything and did my very best? What if you do reach your goal? What if you do achieve your dreams? Who is to say success isn't around the corner?

One night I was sitting at my computer staring at the screen trying to work on my novel. I had just received another rejection and was frustrated with my lack of sales of short stories, lack of progress in finding an agent, and with the mediocrity that was the novel sitting in front of me. I decided then, that I was done writing. I quit. I would fill my time with going out with friends and going to movies and reading all those books on my to-read shelves, (yes, that is plural), and I cried. I wept for my lost dream. I couldn't do it. I couldn't quit on myself or my dream. I hadn't tried everything yet. An hour later, I turned on my computer and I continued to write. A month later, I signed with a literary agent.

I have faced many, many frustrations since, but I know that until I have exhausted every possible avenue, I cannot quit.

In dialoguing with the saboteur, we find out what is important to us in our lives and about what we are working on.

Dialoguing with the Saboteur

My Gollum is a very nasty creature, full of hatred, and he can be incredibly loud. One of Gollum's favorite things to say to me is: "You are so unoriginal. Your story ideas have all been done before. No one is going to want to buy them."

Why is this important to me? Originality is important for a few reasons, least of which is that I have always wanted to have something special to say, to stand out in some way. As a writer, originality is important, without it, chances are that I will never get a book deal.

My response to my saboteur is that maybe I am writing another vampire story, or werewolf story, however, I do have something original to add to the mythology and the elements are unique.

I also like to remember what Brenda Ueland says at the beginning of her book *If you Want to Write: A Book About Art, Independence and Spirit*, "Everybody is talented, original, and has something to say. . . Everybody is talented because everybody who is human has something to express. . . Everybody is original, if he tells the truth, if he speaks from himself. But it must be from his true self and not from the self he thinks he should be." (Ueland, 3-4).

So take that Gollum, I am original and I do have something to say.

> **Step #1 to silencing your inner saboteur:**
>
> Dialogue with your saboteur, find out what is important to you and decide how you will dissolve this protest.

Exercises

Take some time now and write down some of the things your inner saboteur has said to you which have kept you from writing. Don't take too long, just a few phrases.

_____
_____
_____
_____
_____
_____
_____
_____
_____
_____
_____
_____
_____

For each one of those phrases, what is your saboteur protesting?

_____
_____
_____
_____
_____

Why is that important to you?

How will you dissolve those protests?

Chapter 2

Roots

Chapter 2

Roots

Where does the saboteur come from?

In the previous chapter, we talked about what the inner saboteur is and the kinds of things he tells us. Isn't it amazing the lies the saboteur comes up with? But where does he come from? How did it get to hold the power it has over us? Where was the saboteur born and what gives it life?

In order to determine the origins of the saboteur, we need to take a step back and have a look at the evolution and function of the human brain. Once we understand the emotional and creative function of our brain, we can then understand where the saboteur comes from, where and why it was born, and how it then uses that birth place against us.

Our brains evolved in three stages: the reticular brain; the limbic brain, and the cerebral cortex. Each stage of this evolutionary process serves a purpose which is key to exposing the saboteur.

Our Reticular or Reptilian Brain is the tiny enlargement on the brain stem which evolved 100 million years ago. It is responsible for our basic needs. It tells us we're thirsty, hungry, cold, and it is responsible for our fight or flight response.

Our Limbic or Emotional Brain evolved about 50 million years ago, fits over our reptilian brain like a glove, and the two work closely together. This is where our more advanced emotions and emotional memories reside.

Our emotional brain links our physical and emotional awareness, has more sophisticated feelings, emotional impulses and needs. Its development unfolded through group protection and survival. So when we feel threatened, our emotional brain acts on instinct, feeling that physical threat, and puts us in a defensive state. Essentially, the emotional brain is focused on survival, especially the survival of the group, and responds with quick, black versus white, group-oriented actions to preserve the status quo.

To challenge our emotional brain with creativity and change with unknown outcomes, we feel threatened. Our emotional brain reminds us of a time when we were threatened and the outcome was bad for us, causing us harm, and so to protect us, it warns us away from any emotion that might cause the same harmful outcome.

If something happened to us to make us happy, or sad, or afraid, the associations are stored in this part of our brain. For example, if the scent of chocolate has happy, loving associations, our emotional brain is happy, full of love and relaxed. If chocolate has an unhappy, fearful association, emotionally, we remember that fear upon smelling chocolate, and retreat to our emotional brain.

Our Cerebral Cortex is 2 to 2.5 million years old, and is the majority of the grey matter, where all our remaining functions occur. It is also where creativity resides. In order for us to begin, create and finish a project, a story, a novel, we need to be emotionally relaxed and happy so that we can function in our cerebral cortex. The saboteur uses our past negative experiences to keep us fearful and in retreat in our emotional brains so that we are not able to create.

The cerebral cortex works fairly independently of the emotional and reptilian brain systems. The cerebral cortex relies on visual stimulation rather than auditory or kinesthetic stimulation needed by the emotional and reptilian brains. However, for creativity to flow, we need to tap into our emotional brain and connect it with the cerebral cortex. We can do this through visualization and positive emotions. If we can visualize ourselves succeeding and being creative, and associate that with the safety, confidence, happiness and overall positivity, we are able to win over our emotional brain, make it feel happy, relaxed and secure, so we can engage our cerebral cortex and be more creative.

The emotional brain, the part of us that instinctively wants to protect us, that developed out of a genetic need for survival, is the birth place of the saboteur. A specific and particularly hurtful comment or moment in our lives is what gave birth to the saboteur. And it is the saboteur who feels threatened when we attempt anything that might lead us to the same conclusion as that initial comment or moment.

The saboteur then speaks to us in a negative, hurtful, tone of voice to keep us feeling threatened and keep us in its protective nest of survival, preventing us from tapping into our creativity. The saboteur makes us believe we are being kept safe, when in reality, it is controlling us from a position of fear.

To better understand the origins of the saboteur, we need to determine which negative past experience gave it birth.

Examples of past negative experiences

At some point in our lives, someone has said something particularly negative or hurtful which has stuck with us, buried in our subconscious. They have told us we're bad, not good enough, can't do something, can't catch the ball, can't run fast enough, can't play a musical instrument or sing well enough. Maybe it was a parent, or teacher, coach, bullies, and even those ultra-competitive classmates.

Let's look at some examples and then we'll discuss why a particular experience gave birth to the saboteur.

The ultra-competitive classmates: You remember those, in the hallway after a test or exam asking everyone "What did you get for question x?" Maybe they whined that they were sure they'd failed the class, when everyone knew they were the smartest one there, straight A+ student. They probably did believe they had failed the test because they're such perfectionists. They also succeeded in making everyone else anxious about their own grades, if not a complete failure, once they started bragging about their A+ and asking everyone else what mark they got.

Maybe you were one of those ultra-competitive classmates. Unfortunately, I was. I remember a particular report card day in grade two. I lay on my bed crying, it was the worst report card ever. I received a B. Up until then I'd received all As and A+s. To me, a B was the same as an F. I thought my world had come to an end.

In the ultra-competitive classmate, there is an underlying need for perfection at all times. The expectations they place on themselves are often impossibly high. The saboteur is hard at work in these people and their behavior is the result which also affects and possibly infects those around them.

Bullies: Bullies make everyone around them feel bad about themselves. It is what they do. They do it to feel better about themselves and to make themselves look good to others. Female bullies have a tendency to do their job in an emotionally hurtful way, kind of like Gollum, actually, telling you in direct and roundabout ways, that nobody likes you, you are ugly, not worth caring about, you can't dress right, you are too smart, and you are not cool enough. Bullies make you think that there is something essentially wrong with you and everything you are and believe.

Coaches: I would venture to say that most coaches are good coaches, and they have a duty to tell you if you are not up to the playing level which is expected of you. However, here we are talking about the bad ones. The coaches who single out a player on the team and are extra hard on them, or will bench a player, or will criticize a player without teaching them how to be better.

Teachers: Like coaches, most teachers are good teachers, and they too have a duty to give you the grade you've earned. Maybe they were right to give you a failing grade in your composition class. But that failing grade, without any constructive criticism, and I mean constructive, helpful, criticism, such as: there was no conflict along with instructions on how to add conflict to a story, sits in the back of your mind, growing tumors, coming out as a thought that says "I can't write, I failed composition in grade 7."

Family: Families are, unfortunately, the biggest breeding ground for inner saboteurs. Julia Cameron mentions that her students have often used a picture of a parent to represent their Censor. (Cameron, *Artist's Way*, 12). Siblings, particularly older siblings, when they're in their be-mean-to-the-younger-sibling phase, will tell you that you can't play games with them because you are the baby, or not good enough. Parents, because they're looking out for you, will tell you that writing will never pay the bills so keep it as a hobby and get a good education and a good, steady, secure job. Pulitzer Prize winning author Carol Shields told me once when I asked her about sharing my writing with my family, she said, "Don't. Especially when it is a work in progress."

I maintain that policy.

There are some exceptions to the family rule, of course. For some writers, it is okay to share their works in progress with spouses as they often prove to be excellent beta readers. It is important to know your family, and know yourself. From my family, I will only accept the 'Mom critique' of "This is fantastic, you are amazing, the best writer ever." I know I won't get it, I'll get honesty instead, so I don't let my family read it.

Defining the Saboteur's Conception

It can be painful to think back to the source of the negativity in our heads. We need to wade through it though, to find the root of the saboteur. When we remember those negative comments, we are returned to our emotional brain, afraid to be creative because we hear those negative comments in the voice of the one who first spoke them. It is because of that person, that we have developed this habit system of retreat, this need to protect ourselves. The saboteur makes use of this habit to keep us where it thinks we are safest. But instead of making us feel safe, we are left tense and uncreative and therefore frustrated.

By allowing ourselves to go back to that moment and figure out what and who hurt us with that negative comment, we can relax and move out of our emotional brain back into the creativity of our cerebral cortex.

Recognizing that initial trigger will help us to halt the retreat. When the saboteur twists that initial hurt, we again tend toward retreat. Once we engage the saboteur and recognize the triggers it uses and why they are important to us, we can respond appropriately, deal with the issues if they need to be dealt with, and once again relax back into creativity, feeling safe and taken care of, and we are able to stay there longer, and are less likely to retreat so quickly.

When we remember that original comment, the root of the saboteur, we can see how small and insignificant it is which allows us to take away its power over us and silence it. It is rarely just one person who is the root of the saboteur, but of the two or three, there is usually one voice which is most dominant. We will look at that more in the next chapter. In the meantime, it is time to wade back through our memories and find out where your inner saboteur comes from.

If I think back to the root of my saboteur, this is what stands out for me: I always received poor grades in composition classes in elementary school and junior high. It hurt because at the age of seven, I decided I was going to be a writer and had started writing stories. I thought they were all fantastic stories, my teachers apparently disagreed. Now, I don't actually remember what grades I received. I was a nerd in school, so probably if I received a B, I was devastated. But I do remember one of my junior high teachers making the comment about my Halloween Horror story, that it wasn't a story. To this day I disagree. It probably wasn't a great story, but it had a beginning, middle and end, had some horror elements, etc. everything necessary to meet the definition of a complete story. However, the comment that stuck with me was that I don't know how to write.

My saboteur knows how important writing is to me, and always has been. Writing is all I have ever wanted to do. But the writing life is rife with rejection and heartache, which my saboteur thinks he needs to protect me from. Therefore, my saboteur took the teacher's comment that what I'd written wasn't a story, and twisted it, expanding it to everything, telling me constantly that I don't know how to write short stories, or novels, or even this book. Especially this book. Every rejection, no matter how personal, is proof that I don't know how to write. Every acceptance must be a fluke and I am not deserving of it so I'd better keep quiet and hope they don't figure out their mistake and turn me away.

Looking back as an adult, I recognize that the comments from that teacher were specific to that one story, not everything I have ever written. The comment hurt so much because all I have ever wanted to be was a writer. Every comment or suggestion that is even remotely negative about my writing sparks my fear that I will never be a writer.

My response to my saboteur is to first place the comment in perspective. It was specific to that story. Maybe my teacher should have taught me better. Perhaps her comments should have been more helpful. If it wasn't really a story, tell me why and what I could do to fix it.

Then I need to transform this negative comment into something positive. The comment that it wasn't a story created my eternal need to know how to write better has pushed me into pursuing workshops and grad school and to continuously work harder to be a better writer, which will only move me closer to my dream. I can also visualize a time where I have survived all those rejections, I have studied the craft, I have persisted, and the result, the reward, is that book contract.

> **Step #2 to silencing your inner saboteur:**
>
> Look back with some objectivity to those comments which hurt us, push them back into their narrow context, and transform them into a positive outlook and experience.

Exercises

Think back to those times when people said negative things about you, told you you couldn't do something, couldn't or shouldn't write. Write down the name of the person, what the situation was, and what they said.

_____
_____
_____
_____
_____
_____
_____
_____
_____
_____
_____
_____
_____
_____
_____
_____
_____

What made that comment hurt so much?

_____
_____
_____

Take time to respond to each of their comments. Put that comment or experience into context. How can you transform it to a positive comment, thought, or experience?

Chapter 3

The Dominant Voice

Chapter 3

The Dominant Voice

In Chapter 2, we talked about people in our lives whose negative comments about us or toward us became the breeding ground for the inner saboteur. Now we're going to identify which of the many voices on the list you made at the end of Chapter 2 is the most dominant. We will also look at the reasons why it is the dominant voice, and how it has permeated other aspects of your life.

As humans, we have a tendency to listen to the negative comments made about us, and forget the compliments. All too often the negative is more prevalent. Next time you are with a group of friends, observe how quickly the conversation turns to complaints. See how many of your friend's Facebook and Twitter status updates are positive and how many are complaints.

Often when we're asked what our ideal of something would be, what we're looking for in a house, job, or life-partner, we respond with what we don't want, rather than with what we do want. This is a habit that leaves us thinking in negative terms.

As writers, the negative only gets reinforced with those agent and editor rejections piling up, adding to the thoughts that no one wants what you have to offer, your writing isn't good enough, nobody likes you.

Sure, we try to make the rejections positive. You've heard of the "really good rejection" where the editor or agent made personalized comments. Yes, it is good, it is a way to measure progress, someone did take an interest. But deep down in every one of us who received a "really good rejection" lies the thought "I am just not good enough. If they really thought I was a good writer, they would have bought my story/offered me representation/offered me a three book deal with a $50,000 advance."

Gather a group of writers together, and we love to talk about the rejection horror stories. They make for great storytelling, especially from the most prolific and widely published authors. It is also reassuring to writers trying to break into the business, to know that even the biggest names in publishing were not always a success. Stephen King in his book *On Writing* talks about how he had three novel manuscripts completed before *Carrie*. *Carrie* sold first and he did eventually sell the others. (King, 69). Ask any published author, and chances are they will tell you they wrote at least two or three novels before getting that cherished first book deal. As aspiring writers, we thrive on these kinds of stories. They are reassuring. If it took them that long, then I am still all right. But they can also be just as devastating. It took them that long and look at how amazing they are. I am nowhere near their level. I will never make it.

It is at times like these, when you receive another rejection, or are struggling to sit down and write, that the negative and hurtful comments we experienced in our past, come out twisted and disfigured.

Out of all of this negativity, we hear one voice, the dominant voice of the saboteur.

The Dominant Voice

The root of the saboteur comes from a particularly hurtful comment or moment because it hit on something most important to us like our writing, our creativity, or our confidence. The voice of the saboteur is often someone close to us who has, hopefully unknowingly, or at least out of the good intention of wanting us to not be hurt—reinforced in some way that original hurtful comment and the twisted forms used by the saboteur. It becomes the dominant voice precisely because it is someone who is close to us and we know how well intentioned they are.

Remember the teacher who didn't like your creative writing projects? Your saboteur does, and using that comment says, "See? No one likes what you write. That teacher was right all along. You can't write. You should quit." It becomes the dominant voice because we respected the teacher.

What about worrying about offending family? Heather Sellers compares a fear of offending to being clothed when we should be naked. She says, "Sometimes we write as though we are wearing a swimsuit in the shower. Sometimes we are so scared of the truth or of offending people with our very presence, our strength, our energy, our self, that we cover up. We all like to fit in. If the other girls are in swimsuits, well, by golly, we should be, too. Writers: If you aren't naked, you aren't doing it right. If you aren't willing to show your sags, your scars, your beautiful arms, the small of your perfect back – your writing voice is going to keep sliding away from you. It will be clear to everyone that you are faking it. . . A book does not get written when an author fears her own voice, her own perfect body, her unique truth. . ." (Sellers, 162).

Sibling rivalry is also a great source of nourishment for your saboteur. You receive a rejection and your saboteur loves to tell you, "You never were as creative as your brother/sister. Why do you bother trying? No agent is going to sign you, they don't want talentless, unoriginal authors. Your work in progress? Completely unoriginal. Remember the stories your brother used to tell in the car on family vacation? Now those were funny and original. Even your parents liked his stories more than they liked yours. They still talk about his stories." Or it might say, "Your sister was right, she said you weren't good enough for x, so what makes you think you are good enough to write?

Family expectations can also make a strong voice. The saboteur often resides in the identity of who we "should" be, and that identity is often placed upon us and reinforced by family. There may be expectations placed on you to write only inspirational fiction, rather than the historical romance you'd prefer. Maybe you have too many swear words and sex scenes, or not enough. The relatives will be scandalized by what you write, regardless of genre.

I have a deck of cards called *In Their Own Words: Eminent Writers on the Craft of Writing,* by Dona Budd, which I picked up a number of years ago at the Stratford Festival in Stratford, Ontario. One of the cards is a quote from Erica Jong about writers worrying about what family will say. She says "Every woman artist has to kill her own grandmother. She perches on our shoulder whispering, 'Don't embarrass the family'."

More often, family likes to treat your writing as only a hobby, a waste of time. Now that you've decided you want to write, pursue publication, the housework distracts you, family needs distract you, and it feels like everything distracts you because you still believe that writing is a waste of time. Your saboteur is quick to reinforce that belief. Family becomes the dominant voice because so much of who and what we are is connected to and resides within our family identity and our identity within our family.

There may be other comments your saboteur feeds off of. Have you ever heard a famous author say, "If you ever think about quitting or ask yourself if you are a writer, then you should quit, you are not a writer."? This one nags at me constantly. I am one of those writers who thinks almost every day that I should quit. Does this make me any less of a writer? According to some, it might. I don't think it does. My saboteur tries very hard to make me believe this makes me a failure as a writer. The saboteur will use everything to tell you, "You are not a writer." This becomes the dominant voice because the author is a major bestseller, they must be right.

Sometimes even those first 'good' rejections become the voice the saboteur mimics. "Not quite special enough." "Not marketable." "Not quite right for me." The saboteur translates those into, "Nobody likes you, they don't want to read what you write, so unoriginal." This becomes the dominant voice because they are one of the top agencies and they know what they are talking about, they must be right.

However well intentioned the person close to us is, it does not mean their comments don't hurt us. The saboteur uses their voice *because* that person is so close to us, is supposed to love and care about our well-being. When we hear the saboteurs using that loving voice telling us something negative, we retreat back to our emotional brain where we think we will be safe and cared for.

Dialoguing with the Saboteur

To defeat the saboteur and deal with its dominant voice, we need to turn those negatives into something positive by once again putting them into perspective, into context, and give them a positive twist.

For me, the above example of sibling rivalry has become the underlying and most dominant voice. There are others, but this one is the strongest. It bothered me when I was a kid, and it pops up all the time: when I get a rejection, after talking with other writers about their projects which all sound so much more creative than mine, after I finish reading a good book, after I read a book I don't like and I think that wasn't so original, how did it get published and I can't get an agent? It became the dominant voice because it reinforced what the teachers said about my writing: That it wasn't a story, it wasn't good.

It bothered me as a kid because even then, writing was my passion and it was all I ever wanted to do. My brother could care less. He was passing time.

Now here's the catch to all of these negative comments we hear — it is based on our perception of the situation, what has been said, and other people's reactions.

A couple of years ago, I went for a walk with my mom and conversation somehow turned to the story my brother told, which the family always used as a regular punchline in various situations. She said, much to my surprise, that it was such a stupid story, which is why they were laughing. It was a good punchline, but not original or creative. I had read the situation wrong. Of course, it would have been nice to know it at the time, but it does change things for me now.

Likewise, the teachers' comments and agents' rejections may actually mean the story simply does not meet their taste, there may be some need for improvement, or any number of things. It doesn't mean you should give up or that you can't write.

Recognizing that the dominant voice my saboteur mimics is that of my parents', I can take the right steps to silence that voice. I can hear what he says, and as before, I can now with my new, grown-up perspective, put it in its place. I recognize that my saboteur is once again hitting on the importance of the role of writing in my life. Not just that I want to be a writer, but that I need to have skill and talent to be a writer. Do I have the talent or skill? How important is talent and skill in being a writer? After some thought, I can respond and deal with these questions and doubt. There is a possibility that my brother is the more talented storyteller. What is he doing with that talent? Nothing. Talent is only a fraction of what it takes to be a writer. And just because my brother has talent, does not mean that I have none. It was Thomas Mann who said, "A writer is somebody for whom writing is more difficult than it is for other people." Right. So maybe the story flowed easier for my brother, that doesn't make him any more talented or original. As for skill, I've done many workshops, and developing into a better writer is a life-long process. I never want to stop learning and growing in my abilities as a writer.

This does not mean what they said to you doesn't still hurt. Of course it does. That is why it is even more important now, to put that hurtful comment or action into context so that it doesn't become our own negative belief about ourselves for the saboteur to feed on. The past is not your future! Again, pay attention to the tone of voice you and your saboteur use.

> **Step #3 to silencing your inner saboteur:**
>
> Recognize the dominant voice the saboteur mimics, acknowledge why it hurt, and develop a positive response.

Exercises

Looking back over the list you made at the end of the second Chapter, identify which of them is the dominant voice your saboteur uses.

_____
_____

What is the core comment—the root—of your saboteur?

_____
_____
_____
_____
_____

Who or what reminds us most of that comment or experience?

_____
_____
_____
_____
_____

What made it important to you and your thought process about your writing?

How has that statement spread to other aspects of your life?

Put that person, thing, or experience into context and perspective. How can you transform it into something positive?

Chapter 4

Acknowledge Our Fears

Chapter 4

Acknowledge Our Fears

We have discovered the birthplace and home of the saboteur, and its dominant voice. And we have discussed how the saboteur uses our negative past experiences against us to keep us trapped in our emotional brain, afraid to be creative.

The saboteur uses many different methods to keep us from pursuing our creative goals. The critic, censor, and editor are among the saboteur's disguises. Using the voices of friends and family is among it tools. One of the saboteur's greatest tools it uses against us is our own fear. It uses the fear of harm based on past experiences, but even more powerful are the fears it creates in us over potentially real but more often imagined, harmful situations.

Though the process of starting and completing a project, there are four main categories of fear we encounter: the fear of dreaming; the fear of failure; the fear of upsetting people; and the fear of conflict. The saboteur may raise one or more of these fears at any given time depending on the project we are working on. These fears and their sub-categories are powerful tools used by the saboteur. So let's talk about each of these fears, how they affect us, and what we can do about them.

The Fear of Dreaming

This fear pops up at the beginning of a project, creating a fear of even beginning. It convinces you that you don't have the talent, intelligence, worth, creativity or skill, to do what you want to do, to write the novel you want to write. It often arises out of past disappointment. Perhaps the last time you attempted to complete a similar project, the results were not what you had expected or wanted. Now you are trying to keep yourself from having the same disappointment.

This is not a fear of dreaming up a project because we already have the project in mind. This is a fear of imagining ourselves actually creating and completing something, even though it is what we really want to do.

With this fear, the saboteur might say something like, "You haven't completed the other two novels in your drawer so don't even bother starting another one because you won't finish it either." Or, "You already have a novel on submission and it is being rejected by every agent and editor in the business. You haven't sold that one, you won't sell this one."

When we have this fear, we tend to procrastinate, putting off starting a project. Such procrastination only leads to further disappointment in ourselves.

It is time to be inspired rather than be afraid.

When you have a novel or story you want to write, ask yourself, "Why is it important to me to tell this story?" List a few reasons, both personal and professional, that will make spending time on this novel or story worth while. Personal reasons may consist of writing about a theme you're passionate about, a challenge of finishing the novel or story in a certain time-frame, or even completing a novel for the first time. Professional goals may be something like developing better characterization or working on your description, or trying out a different genre.

Visualize yourself working on that novel or story, knowing that while you are working on it you will be telling the story or theme that is so important to you; knowing that you already have the skills within you to complete that project.

Surround yourself with people who will positively support your vision and your project and who will encourage you on your way to completion.

If pictures of failure or road-blocks arise, return your thoughts to the positive results of success and achievement.

Fear of Failure

You may have worked past the fear of dreaming or may have no problem getting started on a novel or story. The fear of failure pops up as you progress on your project, your novel, your story. It tells you that what you are doing is not nearly as good as what others are putting out and that you will fail if you continue, you lose interest, you don't like it.

Even if we do have what it takes to complete the novel with brilliance, this fear has us believing in imminent failure. When we have this fear, we tell ourselves that we cannot complete something because of our physical appearance such as our ethnicity, weight, or age; our economic standing, we don't have enough money; our education, we don't have a degree in writing, we don't have any university or college education. In other words, we don't meet the social standard we think we *should* have. It leaves us feeling powerless to complete the project, and therefore we are unable to work on it at all, least of all complete it.

The saboteur will use the following at this stage: "You haven't taken any classes in creative writing. All writers have a degree in creative writing." "Only middle-class and the independently wealthy white people write mysteries." Or, "Publishers only buy work from authors under 25. You're 26. No one will buy your manuscript."

It's time to dispel the feeling of inadequacy.

If you browse the shelves of any bookstore or library and check out the author photos, you will see that people of every ethnicity, weight, or age, are published. If you read their bios, you will learn that authors come from all kinds of socio-political and economic backgrounds. And you will find that most don't have any writing degree; maybe they've taken a course or two.

Fear of Upsetting People

You are well into the novel or story and you are pleased with how it is going. Someone—your boss, a friend, or family member—decides to give you feedback. Maybe they tell you to change something, or that maybe you're writing too much sex, or not enough swearing (even though it is a middle-grade book). This gives us a fear of upsetting people. This fear convinces you that you will disappoint family, or it shames you by making you think that others will think you are a disgrace or a terrible person by what you do.

We develop this fear when we depend on other's opinions of us for our self-worth. This fear stifles our creativity, often paralyzing us into inactivity because of what others might think about us if we express any kind of creativity or even deign to dream of completing a novel.

Our saboteur will emphasize how disappointed our family will be in us if we write this scene, or take time for ourselves to write, and even make us fear the possibility of bad reviews. He'll say something like, "People are going to read this and when they do, they'll think you're sick and twisted, or worse, boring, and then no one will like you, not even your friends."

Rather than putting the blame on our own imagined lack of skill or worth, this fear puts blame on outside forces. We blame the flaws in our culture, our family, our government, our education system, or our relationships, for our inability to complete our projects.

Let's regain control of our situation.

What are your perceived limitations? Is it that your education wasn't as strong as others? That you weren't encouraged to write? Is it that you've had to work multiple jobs at one time to pay the bills? Are you a single parent? Does your family think you should be doing something else and therefore does not support you?

Define your limitations. Ask yourself what you can do, what is in your control, to get around these limitations.

Fear of Conflict

One more fear gets in our way of releasing our creativity and completing our works in progress. That is the fear of conflict. This is not so much about the project itself, but the time we are taking to do it. This fear pops up when people ask us to help them with something, attend events, or spend time with them, when that is the time we had set aside for writing.

The fear makes us feel bad for wanting the time for ourselves. It convinces us that our family and friends will not understand which will create conflict and because we don't want conflict, we set aside our project to do what is asked of us.

Here, too, the saboteur will use our family and friends against us because we are taking time to write instead of spending all our free time with them. The saboteur will accuse us of neglecting our friends, telling us that soon they won't want to hang out with us, or that they will get angry at us for taking time to write instead of going out with them.

To move on to completion and satisfaction, we must solidify our commitment to our values and to the project.

Write down the importance of and the underlying value in the project. Remind yourself of the skills you have to complete the project and the skills you continue to learn while working on it. Rather than giving a blunt "No" response to requests, are there alternatives you can offer that will require less time, be acceptable to those making the request, and allow you to complete the project? Visualize the completed project and the joy and satisfaction you will have when it is finished.

Working through these fears

The saboteur uses each of these fears to its advantage, to make you believe you cannot write that novel or story. The saboteur wants you to believe that nothing can be done about these fears, that they cannot be removed, or that you cannot move past them.

It is important that we take some time to acknowledge which fear we have. Then ask ourselves if that fear is due to a real outcome, or if the harmful outcome is something we only perceive? Maybe because our family members all work in the family business, we expect that they will be disappointed that we are not following their footsteps. If you speak with your family, maybe you will learn that they are proud of you and want you to be happy in whatever you do. Maybe, once family and friends learn how important writing is to you, they will understand its priority on your time.

If we cannot eliminate these fears, then we need to find a way to work around them. Surround yourself with people who will support you. Stick to the time you have set aside for yourself. Get up a half-hour earlier or stay up a half-hour later to write. It may take you longer to write the novel, but everyone writes at a different pace.

> **Step #4 to silencing your inner saboteur:**
>
> Acknowledge the fear we feel and figure out a way to move past it.

Exercises

At what stage of the novel or story are you?

What fear are you experiencing?

What limitations do you feel?

Which limitations do you blame yourself for? Why?

_____
_____
_____
_____
_____
_____
_____
_____
_____
_____

Which limitations do you blame others for? Why?

_____
_____
_____
_____
_____
_____
_____
_____
_____
_____

List friends and family who support you.

_____
_____
_____
_____
_____
_____
_____
_____
_____
_____
_____
_____
_____
_____
_____
_____

Write down why it is important for you to tell this story?

_____
_____
_____
_____

Write down your personal and professional goals for the novel.

Visualize the moment the novel is completed. Take a moment to enjoy the pride of success. Think back over the time you spent on that novel, what did it take for you to get past the obstacles and limitations?

What did you do that helped you succeed?

Chapter 5

Whispers of Sweet-Nothings

Chapter 5

Whispers of Sweet-Nothings

Over the first few chapters, we pinpointed the birthplace of the saboteur, and identified its most dominant voice, the one he returns to over and over again. Using this voice, the saboteur plants a lot of negativity in us, keeping us from writing.

The saboteur is not always so obvious when it talks to us. It likes to disguise itself. While it likes to whisper venom in our ears, telling us exactly why we shouldn't and can't write, it also likes to whisper sweet-nothings, telling us exactly what we want to hear, telling us it is OK to not write tonight, today, this week.

Listening Carefully

A word of caution, these sweet-nothings are not always from your saboteur. It is tricky to know when they are from your saboteur, and when they are not. At times, our bodies hurt because they are telling us something is wrong. We protest because something isn't right and it is important that we fix it before we can move on. This is a positive thing. It may be inconvenient, and it may prevent you from writing for a while, but taking care of the problem now saves time in the future.

It is important that we pay careful attention to our bodies and the objections. When we listen, we can determine if there is something real that needs to be fixed, or if it is the saboteur trying to distract us?

The key is to listen to your body. When you hurt, your body is telling you something is wrong, you can't ignore it, you need to help yourself. I am a big believer in listening to your body. When it hurts, listen, take time to rest it. Make sure whatever it is gets looked after, from a cold to a headache, to a broken bone or something more serious. Not listening to it will only sideline you longer.

We all have long, stressful days of work, coming home to family and all kinds of responsibilities and when it is all done, we're exhausted. There are valid times when we need motivation and inspiration and time to rest and relax. When is it valid and when is it the saboteur's way of stopping us? Ask yourself this: Tomorrow, will you wish you had written, or will you feel better because you managed to squeeze in a few minutes of writing into your schedule? If you can fit in a few extra minutes of writing, it was a sweet-nothing.

The saying "You can kill more flies with honey" is so true when it comes to the saboteur. I hear the venom/negative whisperings and I get mad. I want to prove him wrong. I have gotten stubborn that way over the years. My saboteur has learned from this and has to find new ways to lure me away from my writing.

When the fear and negativity stops working, the saboteur lures us away with sweet-nothings—a tempting offer of something appealing that I can have right now rather than waiting months or years for satisfaction. These sweet-nothings, though. They come out of nowhere, when I am least expecting them. I hear the sweet-nothings and if I listen too long, I am putty in my saboteur's hands. Rather than giving in, I take those sweet-nothings and turn them to my advantage.

Bitter or Sweet?

Below is a list of the sweet-nothings a saboteur might whisper. What makes it a real issue? What makes it a sweet-nothing? Can the sweet-nothing's be used to our advantage rather than against us? These examples are my Gollum's favorites.

"You've worked hard today, you need a break"

Why this is a sweet-nothing: I am always tired after a day of work. I have no excuses, I have no roommate, no spouse, no kids, and it is so easy to crash in front of the TV for an hour which stretches into two or three hours, because I am tired and I don't want to move. Before I know it, the entire evening, has passed me by and I have not written anything.

Using this sweet-nothing to my advantage: We all have stressful days at work which leave us exhausted and unable to think beyond breathing. On days like these, yes, it is important to give ourselves a break, but not as big a break as the saboteur would like. Take an hour to watch your favorite show or do something which helps you relax, then get to the writing.

"You're not feeling well. Why don't you take a break?"

Why this is a sweet-nothing: I get frequent headaches. Most of the time I can work through them, but it is incredibly easy for me to use it as an excuse to not write. After all, I should look after myself, right? And when the headache is gone, oh well, it's getting too late in the evening, or on the weekend, and maybe it wasn't as bad as I pretended it was, and now another day or two or three has been lost.

Using this sweet-nothing to my advantage: I am a firm believer in listening to the body. When it hurts, it is telling you it needs attention. Call it experience as a frequent sufferer of severe headaches and from having Carpal Tunnel Syndrome for 18 months. If your body is hurting, if you are not feeling well, look after the problem, but don't let it completely take over. Have a nap, take the cold medication, etc. If you really can't write anything, take the time to let your imagination wander, think about your current work in progress. It should go without saying but I will say it anyway, if you are experiencing something severe requiring a visit to the hospital, screw the writing and get to the emergency room!

"Just watch one more hockey/football/baseball game tonight"

Why this is a sweet-nothing: I am an avid sports fan, and while I can edit while watching, it is a lot slower thanks to the frequent distractions of the re-plays. And my focus is split so I am not giving my work in progress the attention it deserves. In the end, either my production is way down, or nothing gets done at all.

Using this sweet-nothing to my advantage: Okay, this really has no redeeming qualities, unless you can write and edit while watching sports. I have learned how to edit, and sometimes write, while watching. I don't have to be focused on every minute of the game but it does slow me down. It is better for me to use this as a reward for accomplishing a certain amount of writing or editing.

"A trip to the bookstore is exactly what you need"

Why this is a sweet-nothing: Do you really need another book on writing? I love bookstores. I can spend hours in them browsing and more than likely buying books I don't have time to read. If I am not in the bookstore for a purpose, I am just wasting time, time which should be spent writing.

Using this sweet-nothing to my advantage: Ah, the bookstore. It can be a fantastic source of inspiration, browsing the shelves to see where your book will be when it is published, finding books similar to yours to help you with the writing of your specific genre, maybe there is a 'how-to' book that is helpful, and finding a book by your favorite author to read. Use this as a reward when you've accomplished your writing goal or as inspiration to remind you why you write, and it will push you back into the chair to write.

"Yes, work on your website and blog and Facebook and Twitter and..."

Why this is a sweet-nothing: Facebook in particular, can be a major time-suck. I am fairly fluent in basic web design, blogging, Facebooking and Twitter. I don't need to spend a lot of time doing the basics. Once I get started, it is difficult to stop because there are always other little details which need to be looked at and worked on and every single one of them demands the highest priority. When I am working on these things, writing isn't getting done.

Using this sweet-nothing to my advantage: As writers in the 21st Century, we understand the importance of networking and social media to get our names out there, to build a platform and a readership. Every day it seems that more and more promotion falls to the authors. Websites, blogs, and other social media sites are important for that promotion and do need to be updated frequently. Designate a specific amount of time a day or week for each activity, and stick to it.

"The writing can wait, why not chat with your co-workers at lunch instead"

Why this is a sweet-nothing: It is important to stay friendly with co-workers, but if lunch time is your only time to write, a quick five minute chat can turn into a full lunch break chat. It will become expected that you will have every lunch with your co-workers. Even if you can block off regular lunches for your writing, if your co-workers are a particularly social group, there's always the group lunches out and birthday parties at lunch, and pot-luck lunches. If friendly boundaries are not set from the beginning, expectations for your participation increase and it becomes a difficult pattern to break, meaning less to no writing gets done.

Using this sweet-nothing to my advantage: If you are like me and you work with a bunch of people, it is always good to be on friendly terms with them, it is networking, it is keeping the workplace civil and happy, and building friendships. It can be hell if you don't get along with your co-workers and the last thing you want is to be seen as anti-social and not a team player. Having lunch with co-workers and chatting with them can go a long way to creating a happy workplace. If your lunch hour is your only time to write, let your co-workers know that you are not being anti-social. Non-writers are always impressed if you say you are writing a book and will be supportive. Do try to strike a balance, though, especially if it is a generally close office. Find some time, even if it is a few minutes, to chat with the co-workers, it can only benefit your career, until that life-changing book deal comes along, or you win the lottery.

"Take on extra writing related responsibilities, it's related to writing and good for your writing career"

Why this is a sweet-nothing: In our eagerness to advance our writing careers and our connections with other writers, in our eagerness to prove we are active members of the writing community, we tend to take on too much. Most organizations are run on the efforts of volunteers, and we all appreciate the work of the volunteers. We want to be a part of it. Next thing you know, you are volunteering for everything or being asked to volunteer for every activity. You don't want to be seen as a moocher, so you do, and soon your volunteer activities give you the great connections, but the connections are useless because you have no writing to share with them.

Using this sweet-nothing to my advantage: Being able to note on your queries and CV that you are a member of writers organizations, that you are active on their boards and in their chapters, means you are an active participant in the writing community. It looks good on paper, and without a doubt, a lot of good connections and friendships are made. Going in, make sure you set firm time commitments for yourself and make sure it is clear for yourself that your writing comes first.

"Just a few more hours of rest is fine, then you can write"

Why this is a sweet-nothing: This is a particularly sweet one for me. I am always tired, sneaking in naps here and there, the longer the better. Get up at 5 in the morning to write? I don't think so. If I did that, then I'd have to go to bed early to get my 8 – 10 hours of sleep a night, so I'll write in the evening. But I am too tired to write in the evening so I'll go to bed early anyway. Sleep is magnificent, far better than taxing myself with writing. I'll write on the weekend, if I can be awake long enough.

Using this sweet-nothing to my advantage: Is this one ever good? I find I write best when I am tired, my brain function has slowed enough that all that can work is the creative part. But if you need sleep, have a 20 minute nap instead of a 3 hour nap. After years of complaining about how tired I am, all the time, I decided to finally listen to my body and do something about it, medically. I still like my naps, but now 20 minutes is enough, and there are days I can go without one.

"Our shows are on, and they'll be great inspiration"

Why this is a sweet-nothing: Sometimes there are just too many good shows, all of them interesting, full of great characters and fantastic writing and then it gets hard to push that off button on the remote control. It is much easier to switch channels until a new show is discovered and it has hooked me and I have added a new show for inspiration that I just can't miss. And yet again, no writing gets done.

Using this sweet-nothing to my advantage: Yes, they can be inspiration and educational, and they can also be a great reward for a good day's writing, or a break from the writing. This was something I learned back when I was in my first year at University and incredibly stressed out. I learned to work on the essays for an hour or two, then watch TV for half an hour, then get back to the homework. It was a great break. It also works with reading. I write for an hour or two, then read for a half hour, then back to the writing. The beauty of today's technology, you don't even have to record them if you don't have a PVR or DVR, or dare I say a VCR, most TV stations play them online for a week or two after they originally aired. Or, if you are so inclined, they do come out on DVD. However, limit the number of shows you watch. I know it is hard, I had to go through the process a year or two ago, limiting it to one drama or two sitcoms a night.

Dialoguing with the Saboteur

When assessing the offer to deal with the sweet-nothings, ask yourself: what is it you want at the end of the day?

I once had a chance to talk with Canadian author Oscar Martens about finding time to write and he said (I am paraphrasing, it's been several years so I don't recall the exact words though this is very close): At the end of the day, would you rather say I did the dishes, or I wrote 1,000 words? Of course, when you run out of clean dishes, clean clothes, and your socks are black when they used to be white, it might be time to do the housework. Personally, I would rather write the 1,000 words.

If the sweet-nothing is overwhelming in its appeal, figure out a way to work it to your advantage, as a reward for accomplishing your writing goal for that day, week, or even the month.

> **Step #5 to silencing your inner saboteur:**
>
> Learn to know when it is a sweet-nothing and when there is actually a concern.

Exercises

What sweet-nothings does your inner saboteur whisper to you?

_____
_____
_____
_____
_____
_____
_____
_____
_____
_____
_____
_____

How does your saboteur disguise itself?

_____
_____
_____
_____
_____
_____
_____

Over the next day or two, and this may be worth tracking over a longer period of time, list the sweet-nothings you hear it say which might lead you to procrastinate in your writing. What do you really need? Is it a valid need, or a sweet-nothing?

If it is a sweet-nothing, how can you use it to your benefit, to get your work done, and use it as a reward?

Chapter 6

The Physical Manifestation or The Symptoms

Chapter 6

The Physical Manifestation or The Symptoms

So far we have talked about what the inner saboteur is and how it manifests itself as that voice of negativity and whispering sweet-nothings. Now we are going to discuss what happens when we allow the inner saboteur to get a foothold, when we actually listen to it. These are the symptoms, the physical, external signs and outcomes, we experience before we recognize we have listened to the inner saboteur. Just like a cough is the symptom of a cold, bronchitis, or pneumonia; using a generic cough syrup may not treat the actual cough. It is when we identify the cause of the cough, we can treat it effectively. It is the same for the physical symptoms that result from listening to the saboteur. We can treat them with all kinds of experiments, we may hit, but more often, it is a miss. We've got to get the right diagnosis to find the cure. The cause of the symptoms is the saboteur and when we recognize that, we can have a longer lasting treatment.

Writer's block

Writer's block is probably the biggest symptom, and is nearly a sub-industry in the writing resource section in your local bookstore. There are books discussing what writers block is, idea books to break writers block, and Julia Cameron alone has a fantastic niche in unblocking the writer/artist. All of these, by the way, are valid and worthwhile.

For our purposes, I am going to keep the definition of Writer's Block simple. Writer's Block is when you are stuck in your writing. It can last a few minutes to days, weeks, and possibly even years. If it goes on for months or years, there might be something else going on besides your saboteur. It happens. Don't ignore it. Do everything you can to figure out what the problem is.

Let's talk about when we're blocked, we're stuck in our writing. We know what we want to write, but we just can't seem to get it down on the page. The longer we stay stuck, the more the saboteur tells us that that we won't be able to get un-stuck and we become afraid. The more fearful we become, the more entrenched in our emotional brain we become. What can we do about it and how will it silence the inner saboteur? If you can figure out why you are stuck, then you know what to do about it and your saboteur has one less method of torturing you.

What is it about your writing that is making you anxious? Is it the business side of writing? Is it the marketability of your work? Is it because you have just received a(nother) rejection? Has someone recently commented disparagingly about your writing or the publishing industry? Are you bored with your writing? Are you bored with the subject? The characters? Have you written yourself into a corner so that there is no conflict?

There is a fantastic book called *On Writer's Block: A New Approach to Creativity*, by Victoria Nelson, which discusses many different kinds of writer's block stemming from various kinds of fears, be it fear of success or fear of failure. Identifying what your fear is when it comes to writing goes a long way to ending your writer's block, and silencing your saboteur who is using your fear to block you. I highly recommend this book, especially if writer's block is something you experience a lot and very strongly.

Perhaps you fear rejection, or success, or fear what others will think. According to Julia Cameron, "Writers procrastinate because it keeps them stuck on one project and allows them to fantasize about the rest, about what they will write when they have the time. This keeps the risk low. A writer doesn't have to write anything until what he's currently writing is over with so if that can just drag on a little longer, everyone can stay nice and safe." (Cameron, *The Right to Write*, 223-224). Not writing and not submitting does keep you safe and protected from your fears, but it also holds you back from achieving your goals.

Often writer's block comes from not knowing what to write, or having tied things up too neatly. Sometimes it helps to go back a few pages or a scene, re-read what you've written, if there's no more conflict and you have nowhere else to go with it, then back-track until you can create more conflict, which leads to telling the story *you* want to tell.

Aspiring writers are not the only ones who experience writer's block. In David Morrell's book, *Chapters From a Lifetime of Writing: A Novelist Looks at his Craft*, he discusses the two times he experienced large chunks of time when he was unable to write. One of the problems he experienced was the need for a perfect draft. He concluded that "…if I didn't strive for perfection, if I somehow just got through the wretched scene I was struggling with, the next scene became a little easier. I realized that I could always go back and fix an awkward scene but that I couldn't fix anything if I hadn't written it." (Morrell, 165) Once he came to this realization, he was able to move on, to write. Another method Morrell has of dealing with block is that if he is stuck on one project, he switches to another. (Morrell, 165). If you can work on more than one project at a time, try it.

The need for perfection. It causes a lot of problems. I like what Terry Brooks says in his book *Sometimes the Magic Works*. He says, "If you do not hear music in your words, you have put too much thought into your writing and not enough heart." (Brooks, 93). What does that have to do with writer's block? What he is really talking about here is that if the story doesn't resonate emotionally, it is because it was written without caring about the story or the character. However, I like this quote for another reason. I find I think too much when I am writing. Thinking about the details of what I am writing rather than allowing the story to flow is where Gollum resides. He likes to weasel his way into my thoughts, distract me, tell me how I should write, and mostly how bad I am at writing. When I shut off the brain, let the heart and story flow, it is easier, often better, and Gollum is silent. I also care about the story, the characters and the emotional heart is back in the story.

When I shut off the brain, the block goes away and word production goes way up. An example of this happened while I was attending a writing retreat in Calgary. I had 4 days to write. Excellent. I sat down, and my hands would hover over my keyboard and I'd think, "What should happen next, what should happen next!" and I'd start to panic. Finally I told myself to shut up and write. Now for me a good day, a full day like a full Saturday of writing, is usually 2,500 words, though I have on occasion pushed it to 5,000 words, but those days are rare. That weekend, when I didn't think, I managed 6,500 words a day.

Something we often forget is that the great thing about writing is that it is personal. No one has to see it until you want them to! So that first draft can be as imperfect as you want it to be. Brenda Ueland, in *If You Want To Write: A Book About Art, Independence and Spirit*, says, "Be careless, reckless! Be a lion, be a pirate! Write any old way." (Ueland, 64). What she is saying is that it is okay to free yourself to make mistakes. Write an imperfect paragraph. Write what you want to write, not what you think you should write. You will enjoy the writing a lot more, and you will have a greater chance at making a breakthrough in your writing because you are willing to take chances, to experiment. Do not be afraid of flawed writing. No one has to see it until you want them to.

No breakthroughs in writing can happen when you are not writing because you are too worried about perfection or you don't feel you have enough time, or that writing that novel is taking too long. Brian Kiteley, who wrote *The 3 A.M. Epiphany*, encourages us to "Be patient. Long projects—novels and even stories—take a long time. Learn how to relax into the rhythm of weeks and months rather than hours and days. It is important to realize that you are probably doing more work than you think you are. From time to time simply take stock of what you have done in an arbitrarily long period of time like a month, and I bet you'll be surprised to see how much work goes into apparently not working all that much." (Kiteley, 250)

Once you relax, stop thinking critically about your work, the writing will come. But be patient with yourself. Ueland also notes that "If you write, good ideas must come welling up into you so that you have something to write. If good ideas do not come at once, or for a long time, do not be troubled at all. Wait for them. Put down the little ideas however insignificant they are. But do not feel, any more, guilty about idleness and solitude." (Ueland, 32-33). Wait. What? What does she mean by not feeling guilty about idleness and solitude? Did she really say that?

She most certainly did! Sometimes writing isn't always about putting the words onto the page. Sometimes our stories require us to stop and think about them for a while. Ueland calls this Moodling, the slow and quiet working of the imagination. (Ueland, 28). She dedicates a full chapter to this in her book which I would love to copy for you here in full, but that would likely break copyright laws. Essentially she says that it is all right to sit, sometimes, and think about the current work in progress. Sometimes, the thoughts, ideas, plot, characters, etc. need time to form before they are willing to be put down on the page. (Ueland, 28-39). It is therefore all right to sit and stare out the window, to let the mind's eye wander. More specifically, she says "This quiet looking and thinking is the imagination, it is letting in ideas." (Ueland, 29). She goes on to say "…the imagination needs moodling—long, inefficient, happy idling, dawdling and puttering." (Ueland, 32). Yes, we do need to allow our imaginations to wander and idle and putter.

Terry Brooks is well known for sitting and daydreaming. His chapter "Dream Time" in his book *Sometimes the Magic Works*, talks at length about how he often sits and thinks out the plot of a novel before he begins to write it, appearing distracted to his family when they try to speak with him. I am sure the saboteur loves to hear that sitting and daydreaming is perfectly fine. We could do that forever! Brooks cautions us, though, saying that "Just sitting down and thinking about writing doesn't always work. It would be nice if it did, but the creative process is more complicated than simply deciding to create and then doing it." (Brooks, 87). So daydream, yes, but then write it down!

Daydreaming is a lot easier than writing. We can daydream any time. Writing, on the other hand, there just isn't enough time to write. This need for time can also create writer's block. If only we could take an extra day off of work. Every writer I have ever met has spoken at least once about wanting a year off to write their novel. And yet, when we have a full Saturday to ourselves, how much writing do we actually get done? It takes a lot of discipline and practice. Julia Cameron believes that "Often the greased slide to writer's block is a huge batch of time earmarked "Now write." Making writing a big deal tends to make writing difficult. . . If we are forever yearning for "more," we are forever discounting what is offered." (Cameron, *The Artist's Way*, 13). The majority of published writers still work at least part-time, if not full-time jobs. It is important to make the most of the writing time we do have. A few minutes here and there are great to keep the current work in progress fresh in our minds, keeping the creative process flowing. Cameron also notes that "When we make time to write, we can do it anytime, anywhere." (Cameron, *The Write to Write*, p. 14).

David Morrell touches on this as well. He says, "Writers write. It's that basic. If you just got off an assembly line in Detroit and you're certain you have the great American novel inside you, you don't grab a beer and sit in front of the television. You write. If you're a mother of three toddlers and at the end of the day you feel like you've been spinning in a hamster cage and yet you're convinced you have a story to tell, you find a way late at night or early in the morning to sit down and write. . . A half hour a day. A page a day. Whatever it takes." (Morrell, 13-14).

It is also quite all right to say no to people who keep putting demands on your time. A lot of people don't understand that writing is work, it takes time, it doesn't happen magically. I tell you, if we all lived in Harry Potter's world, I would invent a quill and ink set-up so that the quill puts my story ideas into the ink and then I dip the quill into the ink and it writes my novel for me, all on its own, and I could go off and do all those other things that people want me to do. I'd make a fortune with that, don't you think? Unfortunately, I don't have that kind of ink and quill to sell you. Sometimes, sacrifices have to be made to pursue our dreams.

Heather Sellers puts this into a different perspective. Perhaps it isn't simply that we don't have time, because we could probably find a minute or two here or there if we were desperate enough. Perhaps the issue is a lack of energy. "You can't write if you're exhausted, distracted, "too busy," hectic, and rushing around. Those states of being push writing out the window. If you're drained, you probably won't be able to sustain a creative life. After all, it takes a lot of creative energy to engage in a conversation, deal with annoying people, make meals, please co-workers, entertain children, and tend to the very elderly." (Sellers, 73) She goes on in the pages that follow to give permission to say no to events and people, to put a priority on your writing. Something your saboteur would not like you to do.

So after all of this, and with the help of friends and a few books on writing and writer's block we've got that part figured out and we're ready to write. The saboteur has not given up. Next he will remind you, as you are slumped in your chair, that:

I don't feel like it

> *"Motivation is like bathing. For it to work, you need to do it daily"* – Zig Ziglar

Have you ever had a time when you sit down for your writing time and you think, "I don't feel like writing"? Which then grows into what's on TV, I need to clean the house, I'd really rather read, I am so tired I really need a nap. All tricks by your saboteur to keep you from writing.

It is important to know what you don't feel like doing. Is it that you don't feel like writing because you are not in the mood for it? Or do you not feel like writing the novel you are writing? If you are bored with what you are writing, ask yourself why, and figure out a way to fix it. And while you are doing that, surprise, you are working on the work in progress, which is keeping your saboteur silent!

Is it because you feel the work in progress is really going nowhere. Is there a way you can fix it? Do you want to? Do you care about the characters? If it is a story you care about, stick with it, figure out where the problem is, and work on it, maybe set it aside, maybe you have to rework it. If you really don't like it any more, stop writing it. Don't throw it out though, you may want to come back to it some other time.

If you are just not in the mood for writing, that's another situation. After enough days of not feeling like writing, what happens when you sit down to write? It becomes harder to get into the mindset for the story or novel you are writing, you feel even less like writing. This is when your saboteur steps in now and tells you you are lazy. It says that if you were a real writer you would always want to write. And then you don't feel like writing and the cycle begins again. Julia Cameron says, "Being in the mood to write, like being in the mood to make love, is a luxury that isn't necessary in a long-term relationship. Just as the first caress can lead to change of heart, the first sentence, however tentative and awkward, can lead to a desire to go just a little further." (Cameron, *The Right to Write*, 33).

So let's break the cycle right now. You are not lazy. Sit down and write a sentence, then two, then three.

But my muse is silent

Building on the lack of motivation for writing is the lack of inspiration or silence of the muse for a reason not to write.

This is another boon to the writing resource section of your bookstore, and an even bigger boon to the internet. There are websites which feature inspirational speakers by key public figures. Other sites show you how to make inspirational mind movies in which you put to music to images of your ultimate goal. Maybe you have heard of the picture or vision board on which you put pictures of your goals so it is in front of you all the time. Some writers I know, including myself, have a file where we keep items which remind us of why we are still in the writing game.

Inspiration is important, we would not be writing if we were not inspired and intrigued by our ideas, but it isn't necessary to get you into the chair. Inspiration is fantastic when it comes, and it can come in unexpected ways. Recently I was at a one day professional development retreat for work and the discussion that morning was on being flexible in difficult situations. One of the ladies sitting at our table, I discovered, is an artist who has been unable to paint for a while. Simply in talking with her, and with other discussions that morning, came inspiration and motivation. Something I had not expected, but certainly welcomed.

Inspiration is fantastic when it comes, but it isn't always there when we need it.

I caution you not to rely on inspiration to motivate you every time you sit down to write. Why? What happens if your editor sets you a deadline and your muse and all your inspirational tools fail to inspire you?

I know, in school all of us at some point left a paper until the night before it was due and pulled an all-nighter, claiming inspiration was at its best then. Was it inspiration to write the best paper? Or was it inspiration to finish it so you don't fail the assignment? Didn't we call that procrastination in school? Julia Cameron says this about writers and procrastination. "A primary reason writers procrastinate is in order to build up a sense of deadline. Deadlines create a flow of adrenaline. Adrenaline medicates and overwhelms the censor. Writers procrastinate so that when they finally get to writing, they can get past the censor." (Cameron, *The Right to Write*, 223). So it isn't inspiration, it is adrenaline that we think we're missing.

Rather than relying on inspiration and an unreliable muse, there are other means for motivation which will keep your saboteur silent. I have a few pictures on my walls which remind me of my decision to make writing my main focus. The pain picture I use is that of an intersection of a few roads, with a sign-post pointing the way to several towns and their distance. When I don't feel like writing, I ask myself which road I want to take, the road to writing success, or the road away from it. It also helps to look back at what I have accomplished with my writing as a reminder of where I have been. By that I mean I look back at where I was a few months ago and how much I have written, and how each successive draft improves. I love to look at the books on my bookshelves, or write in a bookstore surrounded by the books where I want mine to be. A reward system also works. An example would be to write x number of words and treat yourself with reading time, or tv time, or internet game time.

The reward itself is often enough motivation to sit down to get a few more words written.

Pride in yourself for what you have accomplished and what you are accomplishing by writing, is a much longer lasting inspiration and motivation than anything else out there.

External motivation does help. Having a writing partner, someone you are accountable to, helps. A friend and I made an agreement a year ago that I was going to have a first draft done by the time I went to visit her for their local convention. She was going to have her novel edited and ready to send out. If we achieved our goals, our reward would be a hotel room for the weekend. If we didn't succeed, well, I'd stay at her place. It was win-win for me, but I didn't want to let her down, and she didn't want to let me down. We worked our butts off, and achieved our goals. We discovered it is so much easier to let ourselves down but we don't want to let someone else down. We Skype every week and hold each other to our weekly goals.

I am in the middle of a novel, but this new novel is calling to me

This is something I hear from so many writers. Usually the reason given for switching is that they have so many ideas that need to be written and there just isn't enough time in a lifetime, to write them all. Often writers will spend a bit of time writing on the new novel, the first novel gets abandoned completely. But it doesn't take long for that once new and shiny novel becomes the old novel and another newer, shinier novel is calling their name. Sound familiar?

Heather Sellers has a suggestion of how to deal with this issue. In her book *Chapter after Chapter*, she covers this one the best and I will paraphrase here. She says don't go there. Your current work requires all of your love and attention and focus. She says this sexy new book can either be a valid project, or it can be a way to keep you from finishing your current project. She says there is only one way to find out. Take a day or so, and write down everything you can on the new project, then set it aside. Once you've finished the current project, then you can go back to the one which interrupted you. (Sellers, 143-148).

Before you go that route, I want you to pause for a little bit longer and ask yourselves some important questions. You will recall that earlier we spoke about objections arising when something—a desire or a need—isn't being met or has gotten off track. Why are you willing to give up on the original novel? What was it about that original novel that you loved? Why did you choose to write it? What about the new novel is enticing you? Is it the theme? The plot? The characters? In other words, what were you hoping to express with that original novel that you are not doing? What makes you think you will do it better with the new novel? Consider for a moment, before dumping the original novel, might it be worth going back over what you have already written and figure out where you can fix it and make it into what you wanted it to be? Remember, editing is as much if not more of the writing process than writing the first draft.

Maybe there is something deeper happening here. Might it be a fear of failure? Writing is often a painful business. Those rejections hurt. What if you never get published? Are you thinking that maybe the original novel isn't going to fit the requirements of the publishers? Are you thinking it isn't commercial enough? Or that it isn't literary enough? This new novel will be the better one. It will be the one that will make the cut. Now, this may very-well be true, but you owe it to yourself and to your novel, to give it its due and work on it until you are absolutely certain. You may be surprised with what you end up with if you give it enough time, love, and attention.

What other reasons do you have for wanting to give up on your original novel? Think them over, and interrogate each one of those reasons to see if they are true, or if the saboteur is using them to convince you to give up. If your saboteur gets you to give up on this one he will have an easier time of getting you to give up on the next one, and an even easier time on the third one. Starting and finishing a novel is not easy. Maybe it isn't the one that will be your breakthrough. But having a novel finished and on submission to agents and editors is closer to making that breakthrough than having a computer hard-drive full of Works in Progress.

Mood

Mood is different from the section above where we don't feel like writing, we're not in the mood or right frame of mind for writing. This is how we are actually feeling, a physical reaction or symptom to listening to the saboteur.

If we can recognize the voice of the saboteur we can usually silence it before we get to these physical symptoms. It is when we are not paying close enough attention and we've allowed the saboteur to take control that we get blocked, don't feel like writing, depend on inspiration and a muse, or continue to start new projects without finishing any. When this happens, we've given the saboteur power over us and the saboteur's whispers get louder, questioning us, playing on our doubts and fears. We continue to listen and next thing we know, we have spent far more time away from our writing than we ever intended. When that happens to me, I become incredibly grumpy, bordering on bitchy if I am truly honest. I write and I am giddy happy for the next 24 hours. I have heard avid joggers say the same thing. If they have not gone for their run that day, everyone around them can tell.

Diagnosis

When we pay attention to what is really keeping us from writing, we can address the issue with the appropriate cure. Rather than avoiding the work in progress, which is what the inner saboteur wants, return to it, evaluate it, and figure out what you can do to make it more intersting, more marketable, something you want to spend your time with. Remind yourself of why you wanted to write this story. When you spend time on your work in progress, you are writing and preventing the saboteur from controlling you.

> **Step #6 to silencing your inner saboteur:**
>
> Return to your work in progress, evaluate it, figure out what you can do to fix what is keeping you from working on it.

Exercises

Write down what happens to you when your saboteur is successful.

Do you become blocked, watch a lot of TV, let life take over or eat up your writing time? If you have, how do you feel afterwards?

How does it affect you?

___

What is keeping you from writing?

___

Why is writing this story important to you?

List a few possible ways you can make the work in progress something you want to spend your time on.

Chapter 7

What's in a Name?

Chapter 7

What's in a Name?

In the previous chapter we talked about the symptoms of what happens to us when we listen to the inner saboteur. We have also identified the voice of negativity. Now that we know the symptoms, we can cure the disease.

The Unknown

Why is it important to name the saboteur? To put it simply, we fear the unknown.

The greatest horror stories are those where we cannot see or identify that which is causing the pain and trauma. Bram Stoker's *Dracula* was such a brilliant and terrifying novel about a vampire, because the characters did not know what was doing such terrible things to Mina. In the slasher horror movies of the 80s and 90s, we never saw the face of the monster until the end. Bodies would just disappear or be mutilated. In the movie *Jaws* we only saw the shark fin and part of the mouth, we never saw the extent of the shark, but we were afraid. Dorothy was afraid of the Wizard in the *Wizard of Oz* because of his big booming voice and the smoke of illusion. Racism and hatred occur because we fear the unknown Other. We don't know their culture so we do not understand it. We fear it.

As soon as we get to know the Other, a person of a different race or nationality or culture; as soon as we give what we fear a name, know what it is doing, as we now do with the saboteur; because we are dialoguing with it, we no longer fear it.

Van Helsing studied Dracula, he knew how to stop him. Shine a light in a haunted house, we see the mechanics working. Pull back the curtain on the Wizard and you see an ordinary man pulling levers, not a great and fear-worthy Wizard.

In the Harry Potter books by J.K. Rowling, Lord Voldemort is the evil wizard out to destroy everyone, and in particular Harry Potter. Voldemort is so feared by the wizarding community that he is only referred to as You-Know-Who or He-Who-Must-Not-Be-Named. Harry and his friends are encouraged to refer to Voldemort by his name because speaking the name takes away the fear of the thing.

When we are ill, we cannot get a proper diagnosis and way to heal, without naming the illness.

Naming the Saboteur

The same applies to the saboteur. Naming him restricts his power over us and takes away our fear of him. Naming the saboteur is how we begin to heal. Naming the saboteur allows us to confront him and find out where he comes from, what he feeds on. Naming and confronting the saboteur, gaining this new information, you can grow toward and achieve the goals you dream of.

There are ways we can restrict the saboteur even more. Julia Cameron in *The Artist's Way*, recommends that we draw a picture of the saboteur, which she calls the Censor. She says "Think of your Censor as a cartoon serpent, slithering around your creative Eden, hissing vile things to keep you off guard. If a serpent doesn't appeal to you, you might want to find a good cartoon image of your Censor, maybe the shark from *Jaws*, and put an X through it. Post it where you tend to write or on the inside cover of your notebook. Just making the Censor into the nasty, clever little character, that it is begins to pry loose some of its power over you and your creativity." (Cameron, *The Artist's Way*, 11). Naming your saboteur, putting it on paper in a picture, will take it out of your mind and put it in its place, on a small piece of paper, restricted and no longer a dominant force.

As I mentioned in the opening, I have named my saboteur Gollum. I was fortunate to obtain a painting by Andy Serkis, the actor who portrayed Gollum in *The Lord of the Rings* and *Hobbit* movies, a picture of Gollum being captured by the soldiers of Gondor. I have it up in my living room. While sometimes he tries to reach out of that picture and whisper nasty nothings to me, the picture reminds me that Gollum has been caught and is limited. He no longer has power over me. In fact, he's cowering because I have the power to stop him.

Step #7 in silencing your inner saboteur:

Give your saboteur a name, make a sketch of him, create a character sketch, which gets him out of your mind and trapped on the page, a lone, small, insignificant entity which does not deserve the power it takes from you.

Exercises

Don't spend a lot of time with these exercises all in one sitting. Tweak them as you go. But have fun with them, play a little.

Name your saboteur.

_____
_____

Write up a character sketch of your saboteur.

_____
_____
_____
_____
_____
_____
_____
_____
_____
_____
_____
_____
_____

Draw a picture of it. Make it as evil or as goofy looking as you want.

Chapter 8

Challenge Yourself

Chapter 8

Challenge Yourself

We have gone through our past to figure out the root of the saboteur. We have learned to know when it is the saboteur speaking and when it is an actual need to be taken care of. We have dialogued and dealt with the issues and protests raised by the saboteur. We have named the saboteur, giving it not only a name, but a face and an identity. In doing so, we have taken away so much of the saboteur's power over us. The time has come to take more pro-active steps to keeping the saboteur silenced.

Why Challenge Ourselves?

When we accept that editing is very much a part of the process of writing and that developing our skills as writers is a life-long endeavor, the saboteur can no longer use these tactics against us. We must continue to challenge ourselves as writers. There is always something to learn about writing. There is always something that can be improved upon. Ask any well-published author who clearly loves the craft of writing. It does not matter how many books they have published, they continue to attend workshops and read books on writing, because they want to continue learning, developing and improving. They do not want to become complacent. Complacence leads to boredom.

Perhaps you're thinking that by attending workshops, getting critiqued, and reading more books on writing, you're opening the door for your saboteur to step in and say "see, I told you you didn't know this stuff." Well, no, maybe you didn't. Isn't that why you're learning it? So that you do know it? And can use it in your writing?

As you're learning and developing your skill as a writer, you are also keeping your focus on your writing, and how you will incorporate what you are learning.

There are many ways you can challenge yourself as a writer:

Is it productivity you struggle with? Is it getting the words down regularly? Is there a particular area in your writing you struggle with? Are you feeling isolated? Do you need feedback on your writing? Do you need to connect with other writers?

Resources:

National Novel Writing Month
If productivity is what you are struggling with and you want a challenge to write as much as you can in one month, you may want to try National Novel Writing Month, more commonly known as NaNoWriMo. It takes place over the month of November and the challenge is to write 50,000 words of your novel in that month. Their website

offers all kinds of support and ways to connect with others in your area who are participating. But remember that if you want a career as a writer, you will have to write more than one month a year. http://www.nanowrimo.org/

In-person writers groups
Connecting with other writers is so important to keep our creativity motivated. It is also important to receive feedback on our works in progress. After we spend so much time with a project, we get too close to it and can't always see where we do things well and what can be improved on. We will miss those typos and spelling mistakes. A fresh pair of eyes with a different perspective is always helpful. If your town or city has a writer's collective or guild, or other arts organization, they may have writer's groups they can connect you with. Attend local writing conventions and conferences and their literary track of programming and you will meet other writers also interested in forming a group or connect you with someone else who is.

Online critique groups
If there are no writers in your area you can connect with, then the internet is your next best bet. Here are two websites to online groups that have a good reputation. They may not work for everyone, so do your own research before you commit to them if this is what you choose to do:
Critters Workshop: http://critters.org/
Backspace Writing Group: http://bksp.org/

Local writing organizations
In Canada, each province has a Writer's Guild or a Collective. There may also be other smaller writer's groups or collectives in your area that you can connect with. Connecting with local and national writing organizations will provide you with a support system of other writers, and added resources such as writers' groups, market news, workshops, contact information for lawyers and accountants with writer-centric areas of expertise, and mentor programs, among many other benefits.

Other genre writing organizations offering support for writers:
The Romance Writers of America: http://www.rwa.org/
Horror Writers of America: http://www.horror.org/
Crime Writers of Canada: http://www.crimewriterscanada.com/
Mystery Writers of America: http://www.mysterywriters.org/
Western Writers of America: http://westernwriters.org/
Science Fiction and Fantasy Writers of America:
http://www.sfwa.org/

Writer-in-Residence
Many cities and Universities have a Writer-in-Residence program. They bring in a well-published author for several months out of the year and that author is there to provide free critique of your work. Feedback from professionals in the field is invaluable. Check with your local library, bookstore, or University to see what kind of writer-in-residence program they offer and what their guidelines for submission are.

Writing courses
If you find you struggle with a certain aspect of writing, be it description, plot, character, conflict, or many others, a course might be most useful to you. Not only will you receive expert instruction, but again you will be able to connect with other writers with similar experiences. Many writing organizations offer courses or workshops either on location or online. Universities offer creative writing courses through their regular English programs and through Continuing or Extended Education programs. The Odyssey Writing Workshop also offers online courses. Whichever course you choose to take, make sure you do detailed research on what it is you will get out of the class. Make sure it meets your needs, and that you aren't paying for false promises.

Attend writing conventions
Many towns and cities host literary or writing festivals where for a week or two, you get to attend readings and literary discussions. They may also have half-day or full-day workshops with special guest authors. These are a great way to connect with other writers, discover new authors, and learn more about what is being published.

Attend intensive writing workshops
These workshops can run anywhere from one week to six weeks. They are highly intensive with a teaching component and a critique component. They are a lot of hard work but are incredibly rewarding at the same time.

Odyssey Writing Workshop

Odyssey is an intensive six week writing boot-camp. Jeanne Cavelos, former editor at Doubleday Dell runs the workshop and provides indepth feedback on all work. The curriculum is set and covers each aspect of writing. Special guest authors and editors are brought in to teach each Friday, and the fifth week is run by an author-in-residence. Past Guest authors have included George R. R. Martin, Robert J. Sawyer, Terry Brooks, and Carrie Vaughn.
http://www.sff.net/odyssey/

Clarion and Clairon West

The two Clarion programs are six week writing boot-camps. Each week is taught by a well published author and consists of both teaching and critiquing elements. Past author guests include Neil Gaiman, Joe Hill, and Ellen Datlow.
http://literature.ucsd.edu/affiliated-programs/clarion/index.html
http://www.clarionwest.org/

Viable Paradise

This is a one week workshop. Along with one-on-one critiques with instructors, there are student group critiques and daily focused lectures on specific aspects of writing. Present and past instructors include: Patrick Nielsen Hayden, Teresa Nielsen Hayden, Elizabeth Moon, Maureen McHugh, and James Patrick Kelly.
http://www.sff.net/paradise/

Taos Toolbox
This is a two week master-class in Science Fiction and Fantasy writing led by Walter Jon Williams and Nancy Kress. This is not a workshop for beginners. They prefer attendees to have other workshop experience, preferably Odyssey or Clarion.
http://www.taostoolbox.com/

Books on writing
If a writing course isn't quite what you're looking for, perhaps books on writing will help you develop the areas you struggle with. Your local writing organization, library, and bookstore will have several books on writing. They are also available online at online retailers like Amazon, Barnes & Noble, Chapters, and Writer's Digest. Writing books cover all kinds of topics from specific areas of the craft to writing for specific genres to market information.

Read! Read! Read!
Read award winning and bestselling books in your field. Pay attention to the details, figure out what makes that book great, a best seller. Learn from the masters. Go through the bestseller lists and read the books that last a few weeks on them. Each genre has their own award. Find the list of past winners and read them. Even if what you are reading isn't to your taste, evaluate it from the perspective of figuring out what made that book such a commercial success or an award winner. Study and absorb the craftsmanship of the master writers in your field. Compare their writing to yours. Find out what it is about their writing that you admire most and use it as motivation and inspiration to push yourself to achieving the same level of mastery.

Creative writing programs
If you want to pursue writing as an academic program and not just a course or two, several universities offer Bachelor's degrees in Creative Writing. Several also offer a Masters of Fine Arts, or MFA in Creative Writing. Seton Hill University in Greensburg, PA is one of the few Universities that offers an MFA in genre writing.
http://www.setonhill.edu/academics/graduate_programs/fiction

A note on receiving feedback

Receiving feedback on our work in progress is a huge part of the writing process. It is important to have trusted readers who are knowledgeable in the craft of writing to read over our work, point out what we are doing well and where we need to improve. Not only can they point out grammatical and spelling errors, but plot issues we've missed, confusing dialogue, character discrepancies, inconsistencies, and where we need more world-building. Receiving feedback from trusted readers is what makes our writing the best it can possibly be, and ready to submit it to agents and editors.

Having our work critiqued can be difficult and is often an opportunity for the saboteur to work his nastyness. In fact, it can be that fear of negative comments from critiquers and allowing the saboteur to speak, which causes us not to seek feedback. Because critique of our work is so important to our growth as writers, there are a few things we can do to be open, challenge ourselves, further develop our craft, and not allow the saboteur to plant a seed of doubt in our minds.

The first thing you want to do, is find yourself a group of writers who know the craft of writing. If they cannot provide helpful feedback that will help you advance in your skill, there is not much point in asking them for feedback. This does not mean you can only be with already published writers. There are many skilled writers who know the craft, but are not yet published.

Also, make sure that the other writers in your group have the same end-goal. If your ambitions are not aligned, conflict may arise in giving and receiving critique.

Anytime you send your work to someone for critique, make sure that their feedback will be helpful. You absolutely want to hear what you are doing right, but you also want to know what you are doing wrong and where you need to improve. If you do not find the feedback helpful, find other people to critique with.

It is natural, when receiving feedback, to feel defensive. After all, you have spent a lot of time and hard work on your writing, it is your baby, and now someone is pointing out that your baby is not as beautiful as you thought it was. I have an automatic response when I am defensive which is that clearly these people do not get my genius, and more's the pity for them. But I only allow that defensiveness to last for a moment because I don't want it to get in the way of my growth as a writer. Whatever your defensive instincts are, do not let your defensiveness prevent you from being open to the helpful advice being offered.

When you have several people critiquing a piece of your writing, you are free to take all or nothing or some of the advice. It is your story, after all. Not everyone will have the same interpretation of the story and will have varying suggestions. It is up to you to decide the best direction for your story. A general rule of thumb is that if fifty percent or more of your critiquers suggest you make a certain change, you should give that suggestion great consideration.

When you review the feedback, also look at what has not been said. For example, if you receive comments that want to take the story in a different direction than you intended, it may in fact be that you need to make something clearer.

Be open to the feedback, and use it to your advantage, to your growth and development as a writer.

In all of these ways to challenge yourself as a writer, there may come times when the saboteur attempts to plant doubt. By challenging yourself, by growing and developing, you are becoming a stronger writer, you are spending time on your writing, and you are keeping that doubt and the saboteur silent.

> **Step #8 to silencing your inner saboteur:**
>
> Continue to improve your writing by challenging yourself.

Exercises

Go back and honestly evaluate your writing. What areas do you struggle with?

Have you received feedback? What have others said you need to improve on?

What will be most useful for you to improve in that area?

What resources do you have available to you?

Chapter 9

Silencing the Inner Saboteur

Chapter 9

Silencing the Inner Saboteur

When we connect with what is most important to us, the saboteur dissolves. So let's look at ways we can spend more time on and connecting with what is most important to us to dissolve that saboteur.

This is the meat of the topic of silencing the inner saboteur. Unfortunately, the saboteurs will never fully go away. Mine has certainly been active while putting together this book. And like Gollum in *The Lord of the Rings*, he will come back when the going gets rough and try to take over our lives again.

We've got our arguments, we've pinned the saboteur to a picture, we're listening to what we really need, not the sweet-nothings he whispers. It's all excellent and very necessary tools to have in our toolbox. But how do we keep the saboteur at bay?

The absolute best thing you can do is to WRITE! It doesn't matter if it is terrible, that's what editing is for. Write, write, write. Your saboteur can argue that it is bad writing, that you are fooling yourself, but you can argue back that you are writing, it doesn't have to be perfect, you can edit later. You are a writer because you are writing. And the more time you spend with your novel/short story/screenplay, the more you will enjoy it, and the quieter your saboteur will be.

Set yourself achievable and exceedable goals. Achievable and exceedable goals are the small steps you set yourself en route to completing your project. They fit into your daily routine. They are specific, focused on a single task. And they are measurable in that you will know when it has been achieved.

We all have a tendency to think we can do more than we can in less time than we have. With achievable and exceedable goals, we start with small goals that we know we can complete in the time allotted. Start small and add on if you discover you can do more. Make sure you can achieve your smaller goals first, and be satisfied that you have done your work for the day. And if there are days you can do a little more, that is a bonus.

Someone who has never run before is not going to suddenly be able to run a marathon. First they have to learn how to run properly. They build up their endurance and follow a rigorous training program. If you know you have a big block of time to write coming up, train yourself ahead of time to be disciplined in spending increasing amounts of time writing, and continually increase the word count, but don't expect record breaking results instantly.

Once you have your goals set: the big goals, the long term goals and your short term goals, ask yourself if they are reasonable? Do they fit with your life? Keep the daily goals smaller so that you know you will achieve it. Any extra work you do on your project, above and beyond what you had set out to do that day, is a bonus. Build your confidence, know that you can consistently achieve your goals, and exceed them, before pushing for more.

Setting achievable and exceedable goals looks like this: Maybe at first you can only write 500 words a day, or 30 minutes a day, or 2 hours every Sunday. Whatever works for you. We all have a tendency to set unattainable goals. Don't. Start small, build up if you discover you can do more. Make sure you can achieve your smaller goals first, and be satisfied that you have done your work for the day. And if there are days you can do a little more, that is a bonus. Heather Sellers also encourages us to start slow, to set realistic goals, and to ease into the writing. (Sellers, 15).

Setting those achievable and exceedable goals is important so let's take a little bit of time here to develop that skill and walk through the process.

We're going to start with the ultimate goal and work our way down through the steps.

What is your ultimate goal? Dream big here. Let your imagination run free. What is it that you *really* want?

For this example, let's say that we want to be a well-published writer.

That's being fairly modest, not really dreaming big. Okay, I want to be a best selling author with movies and television series based on my books. I want to go on book tour around the world and live in a palace.

We have the ultimate goal. Now, let's think of the one thing or moment that would symbolize that I have reached the pinnacle of success. Believe it or not, it isn't the palace, the movies, or the around-the-world book tour. My local bookstore has a staircase going up to the second floor. Only the biggest selling authors get to give readings from the staircase. I want to be offered to give a reading from the staircase. Perhaps for you it is being featured on the cover of a magazine or anthology. Maybe it is signing over those film rights to Brad Pitt's movie production company. Maybe, like it was for the actor Jim Carrey, it was receiving that first million dollar cheque.

Now ask yourself, what will get you to that pinnacle of success? To be on the staircase at my local bookstore, I need to be a multiple bestseller. To be a multiple bestseller in my genre, chances are high that I'll need to be published by one of the big publishing companies. To get signed by one of the big publishing houses, I'll need to have a reputable agent. To get the reputable agent, I will need to have a marketable and well-written manuscript. To have a marketable and well-written manuscript I can send to agents, I need to have my novel polished and critiqued by trusted readers who will spot not only typos and grammatical errors, but plot and character issues and inconsistencies, and who will help me make this the best book ever. I can't get a novel critiqued if I haven't written it yet. So I have to get writing.

And now for the writing goals. If the final book is to be approximately 100,000 words, by when do I want to have it done? If I think I want to have the book done in a year then I'll have to plan accordingly. The first draft is the most hastily written. At 1,000 words a day, it should take just over 3 months. So let's be generous for extra long work days and maybe a sick day or two and say the first draft will take 4 months. That leaves 8 months for editing, critiquing, more editing, more critiquing, more editing, some more editing, another round of critiques, and some final edits.

Once you have your goals set: the big goals, the long term goals and your short term goals, ask yourself if they are reasonable? Do they fit with your life? If your daily goal is to write for 2 hours every morning before work but you have trouble getting out of bed to get to work on time, you may want to re-think your plan. Either find other times during the day to fit the two hours in, or start by getting up on time for work, then the next week setting your alarm 30 minutes earlier, extending the time each week until you get your 2 hours in. If your plan is to write 2,000 words a day and you have the time to make that word count but you haven't written much more than 100 words a day before, then start with that 100 words a day. Then push yourself to 500 words until you are comfortable with that, then extend it to 1,500 words. But rather keep the goals smaller so that you know you will achieve it and possibly write more as a bonus. Build your confidence, know that you can consistently achieve your goals, and exceed them, before pushing for more.

You will remember earlier I mentioned the four-day writing retreat in Calgary. I spent several weeks prior to that training myself to be disciplined to write for longer and longer stretches of time. I started with writing 500 words a day, then 1,000. While I never expected to be able to write 6,500 words a day, I had enough discipline to sit and write for extended periods of time, and enjoy the writing process.

Ask yourself: How committed are you to achieving these goals? What are you willing to sacrifice to achieve these goals? Remember, it may take years to get a book deal, but when you finally sign, the deadlines come fast and furious, with very little pay. How will you adjust to meeting the annual deadline and still maintain your family life, social life, and work life? What adjustments can you make now so that it will be easier later? You may need to re-prioritize and maybe even eliminate something from your life. Are you willing to spend less time with family and friends if necessary? Are you willing to watch less television? Are you willing to be involved in fewer volunteer activities than others would like?

It is completely up to you how much time and energy you put into reaching your long-term goal, and even in part, the big dream goal. It will take a lot of time and effort. Sacrifices will be made, and you will encounter and deal with a lot of frustration. But it isn't all about sacrifice and punishment. I'm a firm believer in celebrating the little steps as much as the big achievements.

When you have achieved your smaller goals, be sure to treat yourself every now and then. Julia Cameron in *The Artist's Way* suggests we take artist dates once a week, to replenish the creative well. It is an activity away from your writing, that is just you alone, to let your inner child play. They are great, they don't always have to be her idea of an artist date. A treat for me is often a visit to my local bookstore to look at and maybe pick up a small item like a fun pen or a new journal. Other times it is writing time at a coffee shop. Or a movie. Often, it is simply time to read.

A treat once a week is ideal. Never more, it stops becoming a treat then. But treat yourself. Reward yourself. Celebrate, especially the small steps because achieving the small goals means you are committed and working toward that ultimate big dream goal.

To further enable you to achieve the goals you've set, see the Appendices for tools on prioritization, time management, and creating a workable plan.

A final note on goal setting. In this chapter I've asked you to dream big and write down what your ultimate goal and long-term goal might be. For us as writers, these goals are often things like being a best-selling writer, a full-time writer, or having a book contract in a certain amount of time. We want to have these dreams, these goals. Without something to aim for, there is little purpose to our lesser goals. However, it is important to keep in mind that actual publication goals are not within our control. We want to have big dreams to aim for, like a carrot at the end of the stick, perhaps. While attaining them may not be in our control, the goals we set ourselves as steps to put us in a position to achieve our dreams are in our control, and if we do everything we possibly can to achieve our dreams, then we can indeed be satisfied with our efforts and achievements.

> **Step #9 to silencing your inner saboteur:**
>
> Set yourself achievable and exceedable goals.

Exercises

The Big Dream

What is your ultimate goal?

_____
_____

What thing or moment will symbolize success, that you have reached your ultimate goal?

_____
_____

The Steps to Success:

What do you need that will give you that thing or moment at the pinnacle of success?

_____
_____
_____
_____
_____

What do you need to get you to the above step?

The Long Term Goal:

What is the long term goal?

What are the smaller steps that can be taken to reach that long term goal? How much time will each of those steps take?

What can you do each day that will get you closer to reaching your Long-Term Goal?

Are your short-term and daily goals reasonable? Do they fit with your daily life? What adjustments do you need to make in your priorities to make them fit?

_____
_____
_____
_____
_____
_____
_____
_____
_____
_____
_____

How committed are you to achieving the long-term goal?

_____

Chapter 10

Keeping the Saboteur Silent

Chapter 10

Keeping the Saboteur Silent

Writing is the best way to silence your saboteur. Sometimes it is still a struggle to sit down, turn on the computer or open up the notebook, and write. Below are several other ways to silence him as well.

1) Take a few minutes before you begin your writing project, to journal. Maybe you prefer Julia Cameron's method of writing three pages first thing in the morning. Maybe you'd rather journal at the end of the day. Journaling just before you start your writing project is a way to clear out whatever is occupying your thoughts, if it is something to do with work or family or friends, or even your doubts about the writing project itself. Write them down. Get them out of the way so that you can write. You can pick them up after you're done writing for the day.

2) Acknowledge that everyone has a different path to writing success. You don't have to have the same writing schedule as Stephen King or Nora Roberts. We can't. Most of us have full-time jobs and family to look after. Your path is your own. Take it, own it, call it yours.

3) Find a support system to encourage you when the rejections come. They will come. Even well published writers get rejected. If you have a critique group, or even just a group of friends who are writers, they are often your best support. They can also keep you accountable when you are falling behind. As I mentioned earlier, a friend of mine in Calgary and I Skype once a week to talk about writing, the week that was, our frustrations, good news, and we set goals to accomplish that week. We encourage each other, cheer the other one up when needed, and hold each other accountable to achieving the goals.

4) Keep a Smile File, a place to keep whatever reminds you of why you write. Look at it whenever you need to.

5) Set up a routine to help you get in the right frame of mind for writing. I love to watch elite athletes and recognize the routines they have to get themselves focused. All the top curlers have one to eliminate the distractions and make the right throw. Tennis star Rafael Nadal is practically Obsessive Compulsive with his routine: two bottles of water, one sip from each, they must be lined up perfectly, the labels facing the right way, checking out each of the tennis balls, always throwing one back to the ball boy/girl, towels off after each point won or lost the same, his routine has got him to the top of the world of tennis. If you are so inclined to watch sports, watch your favorite athletes and see if you can spot their routine to get focused.

Not all are as obvious as the routines of curlers, tennis players and figure skaters.

If you set up the same routine, it tricks your body and mind into knowing now is writing time, no more distractions. Try to make it a portable routine though. If you are travelling to conventions or on holidays, and you have deadlines to meet, you can't take time off from writing and you will need to learn to write in cars, on planes or trains, in airports and in hotels or friend's homes.

6) If you are working from home or in the same place for a period of time, try leaving your workspace ready for the next day so that you know where to start with your writing, and your attention is automatically focused. Heather Sellers calls this Positioning. She says it is a way to keep the momentum of the project going from day to day and a way to leash yourself to the work. (Sellers, 59).

7) If the thoughts just are not coming, take a walk. Brenda Ueland talks about walking, sauntering along, to get the creative juices flowing. (Ueland, 43). I am fortunate enough to live close to work so I can walk there and home. It helps me focus on the day of work ahead, and it is a great stress reliever after a long day. It also is a great time to turn my thoughts to my novel, to forget work, to think about the problems in my novel and frees up the energy and thoughts to solve the problems. Not just at the end of the day either. When I get to work, I frequently have to send myself an e-mail about the solutions I came up with.

8) Alternatively, if the thoughts or the words just are not coming, get out your journal and write down what has you stuck, what is bothering you about the writing, ask yourself questions about the plot, or

interview the characters to get to know them and their motivations better.

9) Keep the picture of your saboteur somewhere, probably not particularly visible, but somewhere you can see it as a reminder that he is trapped on that page. He cannot hurt you. He has no control over you.

10) When Gollum is too loud for me to quiet, if I have given him too much of my time and attention, I return to the scene in *The Lord of the Rings: The Two Towers*, when Sméagol first tells Gollum to go away and never come back. It is probably a good thing that I live alone, because in desperate times, I will repeat the conversation out loud. It helps.

It helps so much, I have copied and pasted the dialogue below, full credit to the writing team of *The Lord of the Rings* movies, Fran Walsh, Philippa Boyens, Stephen Sinclair, and Peter Jackson.

Gollum: We wants it, we needs it. Must have the Preciousss. They stole it from us. Sneaky little hobbitses. Wicked, tricksy, falssse!
Sméagol: No! Not Master!
Gollum: Yess. Preciouss first. They will cheat you, hurt you, lie!
Sméagol: Master's my friend.
Gollum: You don't have any friends. Nobody likes you.
Sméagol: Not listening. Not listening.
Gollum: You´re a liar, and a thief.
Sméagol: No.
Gollum: Murderer!
Sméagol: Go away.
Gollum: Go away?! Ahahhaa!

Sméagol: I hate you, I hate you.
Gollum: Where would you be without me? Gollum. Gollum. I saved us. It was me. We survived because of me.
Sméagol: Not anymore.
Gollum: What did you say?
Sméagol: Master looks after us now. We don't need you.
Gollum: What?
Sméagol: Leave now and never come back.
Gollum: No!
Sméagol: Leave now and never come back!
Gollum: Ahh!
Sméagol: LEAVE NOW AND NEVER COME BACK!
[Silence]
Sméagol: We told him to go away! And away he goes, preciousss. Gone, gone, gone, Sméagol is free!

11) Most importantly, give yourself permission. This is something I learned while at Seton Hill University. I kept thinking I had to write this serious political fantasy thing that made no sense whatsoever and had already gone through four different versions, each one becoming worse than the one before. All I really wanted to write was a humorous YA fantasy. My mentor, the amazing Anne Harris, saw my dilemma and gave me permission to write my YA fantasy. I had her put it in writing in my notebook. On my graduation, she gave me a permission slip, which I happily share with you. Feel free to make this your own, just replace my name with yours. It said:

"In perpetuity, Sherry has unconditional permission to write whatever she damn well pleases."

I have it framed on my mantelpiece in my living-room. Whenever I get stuck, thinking I should be writing something else, I look at that permission slip, and I am off and running.

> **Step #10 to silencing your inner saboteur:**
>
> Develop a slate of tools you can use to keep the saboteur at bay.

Exercises

Try a few of the following:

Write your own permission slip.

Write out your conversation with your saboteur in which you tell him to be quiet and get out of your life.

Connect with a fellow writer who can be your accountability partner. Find whatever method or methods work best for you and write them down.

Conclusion

Conclusion

It is hard to believe we have come to the end. We have done a lot of good work beginning with knowing where the saboteur comes from, how to dialogue with it, work our way around it, and dissolve it. We can now distinguish between the saboteur and an actual need. Most important, we have our own tools to keep the saboteur silent.

As you move on toward achieving your goals, remind yourself, when necessary, the steps to silencing your inner saboteur.

The steps to silencing the inner saboteur are:

1. Dialogue with your saboteur, find out what is important to you and decide how you will dissolve this protest.

2. Look back with some objectivity to those comments which hurt us, push them back into their narrow context, and transform them into a positive outlook and experience.

3. Recognize the dominant voice the saboteur mimics, acknowledge why it hurt and develop a positive response.

4. Acknowledge the fear we feel and figure out a way to move past it.

5. Learn to know when it is a sweet-nothing and when there is actually a concern.

6. Return to your work in progress, evaluate it, figure out what you can do to fix what is keeping you from working on it.

7. Give your saboteur a name, makr a sketch of him, create a character sketch, which gets him out of your mind and trapped on the page, a lone, small, insignificant entity which does not deserve the power it takes from you.

8. Continue to improve your writing by challenging yourself.

9. Set yourself achievable and exceedable goals.

10. Develop a slate of tools you can use to keep the saboteur at bay.

You are capable of being the best version of yourself and that you already have all the resources you need within yourself to get whatever you truly want. By silencing your inner saboteur, you are freeing yourself to express yourself, your creativity and originality. You are taking great leaps toward achieving your goals and success as a writer. You can be proud of all your accomplishments and all your hard work.

Silencing the inner saboteur is an on-going process. As with everything else, the more you work at it, the easier it becomes. I encourage all of you to keep up with the journaling and keeping track of your saboteur's whispers. Don't dwell on the negativity. Turn those negative past experiences into positive adventures of possibility. Focus on who you are, what you want, and what is most important to you. Surround yourself with supportive people. Visualize your successful achievement of your goal and think about all the positive things you did and that happened to get you to that point.

A final note. You may have notice that throughout this book I talk about rewarding yourselves. In psychology, they refer to this as positive reinforcement and it is a great way to encourage the beavior we want, which in this case, is writing. I just believe we respond better to reward rather than unishment. Wouldn't you rather sit down and write if you knew there was a treat waiting for you at the end of it, instead of writing to avoid something bad?

I'm also a believer in celebrating the small steps. Especially the small steps. As I mentioned in chapter 9, the small steps are proof of our commitment. They are also done in private and are a lot of hard work that few people will ever see. If we don't celebrate them, no one else will.

And finally, one of the most important things I ever learned from my classmates at Seton Hill University is to believe in myself. And so I encourage you to do the same. Believe that you have something to say. Believe that the world wants to read your work. Believe that the world needs to read your work.

I want to leave you with a quote from Terry Brooks which I keep as my screensaver at home. Terry Brooks says, "Writing is life. Breathe deeply of it." (Brooks, 197). And Stephen King says, "Writing is magic, as much the water of life as any other creative art. The water is free. So drink. Drink and be filled up." (King, 275).

Appendices

Appendices

Sometimes we need a few extra tools to achieve our goals. We have day jobs, family, friends, and other responsibilities that have claims on our time. The following three appendices are some more tools we use in coaching to help our clients reach their goals.

A. *Prioritization* – This tool is to help determine the activities which are most important in your life and your goal. Determining those priorities will help put them in their rightful place in the daily schedule. It will also help determine which events are necessary to every-day living which can possibly be deferred, delegated, dumped, reorganized, or done to get off the list and make room for our goal-oriented priorities.

B. *Time Management* – Once those goal-oriented priorities are identified, they still need to fit into our daily schedule. This tool is to help do just that. By looking at all that is demanded of our time, to work out where we can shift things around, to make room for the goal-oriented priorities.

C. *Creating a Workable Plan* – This is a simple tool, just a few basic questions you can ask and re-ask yourself as you work through the process of achieving each of your goals. I've listed them in a specific order, but you can re-arrange them as you like. But do answer all of the questions.

Appendix A

Prioritization

If you find that you are struggling to find the time to work writing into your schedule, it may be a matter of re-arranging your priorities. When we list the priorities in our life, what we are spending our time on, we can determine which activities are most important to the pursuit of our goals, which ones are necessary to our every-day survival, which ones can be deferred, delegated, and which ones can be dismissed all together.

The first thing to do is list your ultimate goal, be it completing a short story, novel, getting published, having a career as a novelist, or whatever it might be.

The Ultimate Goal:
_____
_____

Next, write down the activities that are important to achieving your goal. These activities are things like writing, reading, research, writing, and did I mention writing?

_____
_____
_____
_____
_____
_____
_____
_____

Then write down activities which must be done now. These don't have anything to do with your goal, but are necessary to your survival, such as eating meals, going to work, paying bills, and looking after the kids. These are often more demanding of our time than the activities that will get us closer to achieving our goals.

_____
_____
_____
_____
_____
_____

Finally list the activities that are neither urgent nor important, but what we spend our time on. These activities include watching TV, playing computer games; things that we spend our time on to relax or procrastinate. Those sweet-nothings the saboteur lures us with.

_____
_____
_____
_____
_____

Now that you have these activities listed, ask yourself the following questions:

Where am I spending too much time?

_____
_____
_____
_____
_____

Where am I spending too little time?

_____
_____
_____
_____

Where are the time opportunities in my life? Early morning, lunch time, writing while dinner is in the oven?

Which parts of my day are most productive? Why?

Which parts of my day are least productive? Why?

What or who controls my time?

_____
_____
_____
_____

How can I gain this control back?

_____
_____
_____
_____

What or who causes the most interruptions in my day?

_____
_____
_____
_____

How can these be controlled or eliminated?

___

What patterns in my day can be altered for the benefit of reaching my goal?

___

What do I do that could be eliminated from my schedule?

___

What activity do I do that could be delegated or shared with others?

_____
_____
_____
_____
_____

When we make writing a greater priority, we become more dismissive of the saboteur and it has less control over us.

Appendix B

Time Management

You've made writing a priority, but you're still having difficulty making time in your day or week for writing. You've gone through your regular activities and figured out which are more important than others, which are more urgent than others. Maybe you don't have the resources to delegate or dismiss certain activities which, if you could, would make spending time on your goals much easier.

Take a week or two and keep track of how you spend your time. Don't judge yourself, don't change things to be what you think you should be doing, unless it fits naturally.

Review your time log. Look at the activities you spend your time on. Do you spot any patterns?

_____
_____
_____
_____
_____

Review your goal and priorities. How would you like to spend your time in relation to your goal—the long term goal and short term goals?

_____
_____
_____
_____
_____

Prepare a timeline that will help achieve the goals you've outlined. Draw a timeline with today as the starting point and the completion of the novel as the end point. Write down when you want to have your short-term goals done to achieve your long-term goal. At this point, don't look at your time log.

Now compare your ideal timeline with your current use of time. Examine the gaps, discrepancies, and overlaps between the two. This will pinpoint the differences between your current use of time and your intended use of time. What are the reasons for the differences?

_____
_____
_____
_____
_____
_____
_____
_____
_____
_____
_____
_____

Mesh the current use of time with the ideal timeline to create a realistic, workable timeline.

Test out this new timeline for a week or two. Then evaluate how well it worked. Fix what needs to be fixed.

As you review what you spend your time on, are there activities that can be eliminated?

_____
_____
_____
_____
_____
_____
_____
_____
_____

When we have reasonable expectations of our time and can work writing into our schedules and it fits well, it becomes a natural part of our lives, rather than an unsustainable activity with too much stress. The saboteur will then have less to hold against you because you are working toward your goal.

Appendix C

Creating a Workable Plan

One more tool we can use to silence the inner saboteur is to have an over-all plan for the novel or short story. This plan is developed using the basic questions of where, when, what, whose, how, why, and who? Sometimes it helps to answer these questions in order in one direction, or in the other, and sometimes to ask them in a more random order, whichever way works best for you to create the plan.

What do I mean by answering questions in a particular order? The questions break down like this: the first level of questions are the environmental questions of where and when. Once you have answered the environmental questions, then we can move up to the behavior and action questions of what and whose. Then we move up to the question of capabilities which is how. And then to the values question of why. And finally, to the identity question of who. We can then take it one more step further to the vision question of who else.

You will notice that these same questions have been asked throughout this book.

More specifically, let's look at the questions we need to answer to develop this working plan for our novel or story, or writing career.

The Environment Questions: When do you want to begin this novel? When will you sit down and start writing? When will you be able to schedule your writing time? Where will you do your best writing?

The Behavior Questions: What do you want to change about your schedule to be able to achieve your writing goal? What small steps will you set for yourself that will help you achieve your goal?

The Capabilities Questions: What writing resources do you have available to you? How will you make this goal happen?

The Values Questions: Why is writing important to you? Why is this story important to you? Why do you want to be a writer?

The Identity Questions: Who are you being as a writer? Who do you want to be?

The Vision Question: Who else is affected by you being a writer? How will your writing benefit others?

Some people find it easier to think about who they are being as a writer first, then work their way down to the more specific questions of capabilities on down to environment. At other times, it is easier to start with the essential questions of when and where, then move up into the more idealistic questions of values and identity. It is up to you.

An example then, of how this writing plan would look:

Environment: I want to begin this novel tonight, and I want to have it finished and ready for submission in one year. I will start writing tomorrow morning, starting at 6:00 am before the kids get up. I will write for 90 minutes each morning, or 1,000 words a day. And I will write curled up on my la-z-boy in front of the fireplace with a warm cup of coffee next to me.

Behavior: I am going to get up 90 minutes earlier each day, which means going to bed earlier. I can PVR "The Daily Show". I will write daily, and I will stop my inner saboteur from criticizing me all the time by writing. I will also have my permission form to myself on my desk so I can look at it whenever I get frustrated.

Capabilities: I have all the abilities I need to be able to write the novel I need to write. I will become a member of my local writer's guild and join a critique group. If I need more writing books, I have a local bookstore I can go to, and a library with resources. I will also look into online classes I can take to work on my character arc issues.

Values: Writing is important to me because it is my life, it is all I have ever wanted. Writing is important to me because I believe I have something to say. This story is important to me because its theme is human rights, and issue I am passionate about.

Identity: When I am writing, I am expressing my creativity, I have a voice, I have something important to say. When I am writing, I am being myself, the person I was meant to be. I want to be published by one of the big traditional publishers, and I want to be respected by my peers and by readers.

Vision: My friends and family will be the most immediately affected because I won't be able to spend as much time with them. When my book is published, they will be proud of me. When I am writing, they will see how happy I am. And when I am happy, I am kinder and more generous and that will benefit them. When I am being who I want to be, I will be more able to help my family and friends when they need me. When my book is published, the readers will be affected by hearing what I have to say. I will also be giving voice to the issue of human rights.

The Environment Questions: When do you want to begin this novel? When will you sit down and start writing? When will you be able to schedule your writing time? Where will you do your best writing?

The Behavior Questions: What do you want to change about your schedule to be able to achieve your writing goal? What small steps will you set for yourself that will help you achieve your goal?

The Capabilities Questions: What writing resources do you have available to you? How will you make this goal happen?

The Values Questions: Why is writing important to you? Why is this story important to you? Why do you want to be a writer?

The Identity Questions: Who are you being as a writer? Who do you want to be?

_____
_____
_____
_____
_____
_____
_____
_____
_____

The Vision Question: Who else is affected by you being a writer? How will your writing benefit others?

_____
_____
_____
_____
_____
_____
_____
_____
_____

Resources

Resources

If you want to go further into this topic (but don't let it take away from your writing time!), I highly recommend the following which I have used throughout this book, or highly recommend reading.

Books

Atkinson, Marilyn & Chois, Rae T. *Inner Dynamics of Coaching*. Canada: Exalon Publishing Ltd, 2007.

— *Step-by-Step Coaching*. Canada: Exalon Publishing Ltd, 2007.

Brooks, Terry. *Sometimes the Magic Works: Chapters from a Writing Life*. New York, New York: Del Rey Books, 2003.

Cameron, Julia. *The Artist's Way: A Spiritual Path to Higher Creativity, Tenth Anniversary Edition*. New York, New York: Jeremy P. Tarcher/Putnam, 1992, 2002.

— *The Right to Write: An Invitation and Initiation in the Writing Life*. New York, New York: Jeremy P. Tarcher/Putnam, 1998.

— *The Writer's Life: Insights from The Right to Write*. New York, New York: Jeremy P. Tarcher/Putnam, 2001.

Dickinson, Arlene. *Persuasion: A New Approach to Changing Minds*. Toronto, Canada: Harper Collins Publishers Ltd, 2011.

Heffron, Jack. *The Writer's Idea Book How to Develop Great Ideas for Fiction, Nonfiction, Poetry and Screenplays*. Cincinnati, Ohio: Writer's Digest Books, 2000.

King, Stephen. *On Writing: A Memoir of the Craft*. New York, New York: Pocket Books, 2000.

Kiteley, Brian. *The 3 A.M. Epiphany: Uncommon Writing Exercises That Transform Your Fiction*. Cincinnati, Ohio: Writer's Digest Books, 2005.

McAteer, Andrew. *The 101 Habits of Highly Successful Novelists: Insider Secrets from Top Writers*. Avon, Massacheusettes: Adams Media, 2008.

Morrell, David. *Chapters from a Lifetime of Writing: A Novelist Looks at his Craft*. Cincinnati, Ohio: Writer's Digest Books, 2002.

Nelson, Victoria. *On Writer's Block: A New Approach to Creativity*. New York, New York: Houghton Mifflin company, 1993.

Sellers, Heather. *Chapter after Chapter*. Cincinnati, Ohio: Writer's Digest Books, 2007.

Ueland, Brenda. *If You Want to Write: A Book About Art, Independence and Spirit*. Saint Paul, Minnesota: Graywolf Press, 1987.

Movies

The Lord of the Rings: The Two Towers Special Extended DVD Edition. Peter Jackson, Dir. New Line Home Entertainment, 2003.

Websites

Lane Robins - www.lanerobins.com/main/index.php
Odyssey Writing Workshop - www.sff.net/odyssey/
Seton Hill University – www.setonhill.edu
Sherry's Website – http://sherrypeters.wordpress.com

About the Author

Sherry Peters lives in Winnipeg, where she works as a Life Coach for students at St John's College at the University of Manitoba, and her evenings and weekends writing. Sherry is a trained Life Coach specializing in the areas of creativity and career transition. She attended the Odyssey Writing Workshop and earned her M.A. in Writing Popular Fiction from Seton Hill University. She credits the year she spent in Northern Ireland as not only being one of the best years of her life, but for being a daily inspiration and motivation in her writing. For more information on Sherry, her coaching, *Silencing Your Inner Saboteur,* and when Sherry will be presenting her workshops, visit her website at http://sherrypeters.wordpress.com.

www.ingramcontent.com/pod-product-compliance
Lightning Source LLC
Chambersburg PA
CBHW031416290426
44110CB00011B/401